T0339721

Cambridge Elements ≡

Elements in Critical Heritage Studies
edited by
Kristian Kristiansen, *University of Gothenburg*
Michael Rowlands, *UCL*
Francis Nyamnjoh, *University of Cape Town*
Astrid Swenson, *Bath University*
Shu-Li Wang, *Academia Sinica*
Ola Wetterberg, *University of Gothenburg*

HERITAGE AND DESIGN

Ten Portraits from Goa (India)

Pamila Gupta
University of the Witwatersrand

CAMBRIDGE
UNIVERSITY PRESS

Shaftesbury Road, Cambridge CB2 8EA, United Kingdom

One Liberty Plaza, 20th Floor, New York, NY 10006, USA

477 Williamstown Road, Port Melbourne, VIC 3207, Australia

314–321, 3rd Floor, Plot 3, Splendor Forum, Jasola District Centre, New Delhi – 110025, India

103 Penang Road, #05–06/07, Visioncrest Commercial, Singapore 238467

Cambridge University Press is part of Cambridge University Press & Assessment, a department of the University of Cambridge.

We share the University's mission to contribute to society through the pursuit of education, learning and research at the highest international levels of excellence.

www.cambridge.org
Information on this title: www.cambridge.org/9781108744171

DOI: 10.1017/9781108881579

First published 2022

A catalogue record for this publication is available from the British Library.

ISBN 978-1-108-74417-1 Paperback
ISSN 2632-7074 (online)
ISSN 2632-7066 (print)

Heritage and Design

Ten Portraits from Goa (India)

Elements in Critical Heritage Studies

DOI: 10.1017/9781108881579
First published online: August 2022

Pamila Gupta
University of the Witwatersrand

Author for correspondence: Pamila Gupta, pamila.gupta@wits.ac.za

Abstract: This Element looks at the relationship between heritage and design by way of a case-study approach. It offers up ten distinct portraits of a range of heritage makers located in Goa, a place that has been predicated on its difference, both historical and cultural, from the rest of India. The author attempts to read the heritage of Goa – a former Portuguese colonial enclave (1510–1961) surrounded by what was previously British India (1776–1947) – as a form of place-ness, a source of inspiration for further design work that taps into the Goa of the twenty-first century. The series of portraits is visual, literary, and sensorial and takes the reader on a heritage tour through a design landscape of villages, markets, photography festivals, tailors and clothing, books, architecture, painting, and decorative museums. It does so in order to explore heritage futures as increasingly dependent on innovation, design, and the role of the individual.

Keywords: heritage, design, Goa, hinterland, village

ISBNs: 9781108744171 (PB), 9781108881579 (OC)
ISSNs: 2632-7074 (online), 2632-7066 (print)

*To my worldly parents: Indra Narayan Gupta (1935–2020)
and Sukarma Gupta (1937–2022)*

Contents

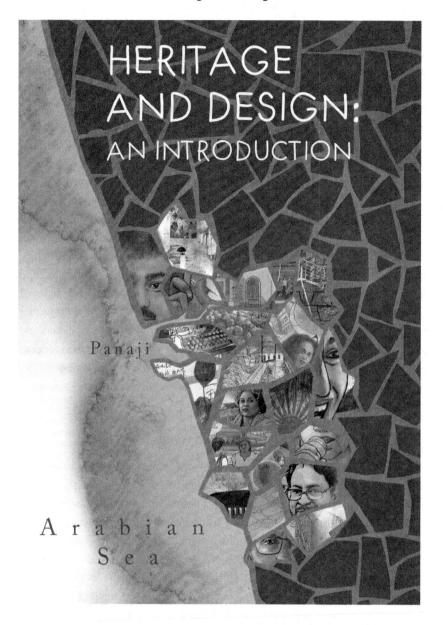

Illustration by Orijit Sen, Goa. Copyright 2022.

We restate the question: can design be reoriented from its dependence on the marketplace toward creative experimentation with forms, concepts, territories, and materials, especially when appropriated by subaltern communities struggling to redefine their life projects in a mutually enhancing manner with the Earth?

(Arturo Escobar, Designs for the Pluriverse, xvii)

1 Heritage and Design: An Introduction

This Element proposes to look at the relationship between heritage and design by way of a case-study approach based in contemporary India. I offer up ten distinct portraits of a range of heritage makers located in Goa, a place that has been predicated on its difference, both historical and cultural, from the rest of India (Gupta 2009b) over the longue durée. For the first-time visitor to this tropical paradise situated on the edge of the Indian Ocean, it is a site of monsoonal beaches, ageing European hippies, Russian package tourists, Indian elites and honeymooners, Portuguese Catholic architecture, and its now-famous Goan prawn curry and rice (Gupta 2014a). For the long-time resident who moves away from the beach and enters its hinterland, it is a space for a range of innovative heritage design projects (Gupta 2018b). I attempt to read the distinct heritage of Goa – a former Portuguese colonial enclave (1510–1961) surrounded by what was previously British India (1776–1947) – as a form of place-ness, as a source of inspiration for further design work that taps into Goa of the twenty-first century. My series of portraits is visual, literary, and sensorial and takes the reader on a heritage tour through a design landscape of villages, markets, photography festivals, tailors and clothing, books, architecture, painting and decorative museums. I do so in order to explore heritage and its future iterations as increasingly dependent on innovation, design, and the role of the individual but also always as a member of a heritage community.

1.1 Conceptual Framing: Heritage and Design

This Element is rooted in ethnographic ways of seeing and writing in order to think through the relationship between heritage and design, an underdeveloped area within heritage studies (Meurs 2016). I am also interested in thinking about a heritage's place-ness as a laboratory for different design projects and practices, with acts of design involving dimensions of training and expertise, skill and labour, specialized craft and industry, commitments (to ideas and places), and judgements or dispositions in particular ways (Sennett 2008; Adamson 2010; Meurs 2016). For the case in hand, I explore how certain practitioners of design (for example, architects, urban planners, photography and museum curators, writers and publishers, fashion designers, and painters) use a specific heritage site (involving its signature details of history and culture) as a source of inspiration for other kinds of aesthetic work involving the old and new, the experiential and affective. I then examine the multiple ways these ideas get translated into material heritage objects (be it a building, book, article of clothing, photo display, painting, museum exhibit). While some of these are more classic design subjects (such as architecture or clothing), others are new ones (such as photography, the book, or a market), which perhaps require more careful thinking about the design work put into each different heritage project, as I do in the sections that follow. I also hope to complicate the distinction between 'greater' and 'lesser' heritage (Butler 2016) by way of design to open up both the range of heritagization processes that are taking place in Goa and what can be considered under the rubric of 'heritage' more generally. Lastly, these processes require thinking about the ethics of responsibility (to both heritage and design) in doing. The heritage makers I profile were selected precisely for their thought, care, and commitment to Goa as a space and place. In other words, it is not simply the transformation of something old by way of new design ideas that defines heritage, it is rather about the biography of the individual involved and their changing relationship to Goa over a lengthy period that show a more dynamic and performative heritage landscape in the making. Furthermore, and not surprisingly, these same persons know and respect one another, often through their design work, and make up a heritage community of sorts, one committed to Goa's continued and sustainable heritagization.

Ethnography becomes my entry point into their life worlds and design ideas and practices; here, I conceive it as a form of design, or 'specialized craft' (Andrews 2009), involving a set of multiple methodologies that I have put together. First, it involves traditional anthropological fieldwork technologies such as conducting life histories and interviews alongside participant observation. Secondly, it is fieldwork that takes place over the longue durée through multiple timed visits, which, in turn, reveals both changes in Goa's heritage-scape and the creative changing practices of this set of heritage makers. There is also an auto-ethnographic dimension to this long-term engagement that reveals my own set of changing research topics and personal relationships to these heritage practitioners. Thirdly, it involves spatial and visual mapping and close study of design projects, building towards what is a growing subfield in the discipline, 'design anthropology' (Mazzarella 2003; www.culanth.org/field-sights/series/keywords-for-ethnography-and-design). It is a way, according to pioneering figure Dori Tunstall, of seeing design as translating values into tangible objects and experiences ('Design Anthropology: What can designers learn from anthropologists?' www.abc.net.au/radionational/programs/archived/bydesign/2008-08-23/3200730). Fourthly, my ethnographic design equally involves online digital research, an expanding arena for gathering data (Hine 2000; Horst and Miller 2012), including interviews, extracts, and visual content and websites often designed by these individual heritage practitioners themselves; they are also integral to the fieldwork process. In other words, the in-person and online supplement one another (through shared content and connection) through what has recently been called a 'multimodal' approach (Chin 2017; Collins, Durington, and Gill 2017; Dattatreyan and Marrero-Guillamon 2019). Together, they create and perform a lively heritage personality and presence and very much form part of the appeal to a larger Goan global community that has a long history of diaspora-making with connections to multiple elsewheres (Gupta 2019c, Frenz 2014). Specifically, my research will suggest that the online increasingly functions as its own design studio space, an important and crucial feature that contributes to the overall design project, so that Goa's heritagization is showcased both locally and globally. My particular 'patch-work ethnography' (www.culanth.org/fieldsights/a-manifesto-for-patchwork-ethnography) then is one of combining long-term classical anthropological fieldwork methods (and timed multiple visits), with encounters and writings of self, design foci, and online research; it is also one that is derived from and tailored to the specific heritage space and place of Goa.

Moreover, there are several interesting historic parallels at work here throughout the research-design format. One is between my changing relation-ship with Goa, starting from the cusp of the twenty-first century through its first two decades, and Goa's changing relationship with the expansion of the Internet over this same time frame, and its increasing role in Goa's fashioning of itself for a global Goan diasporic and world audience. A second is that it is as much about Goa's making itself into a heritage destination as it is about the designing of heritage that is required to make it sustainable, timely, and relevant, and which it builds and carefully crafts, including its digital lifeworlds. A third parallel is that of my own ethnography as a form of research design operating in simultaneity to Goa designing its sense of self and its heritage landscape; both are in flux and always dynamic, always relational.

This Element also exposes the globality of Global South locations such as Goa (India) (Gupta et al. 2018, Connell 2007) and showcases a range of dynamic heritage practitioners who are contributing distinct formations of globality through their design objects, sites, and practices. We could also see these heritage design projects as practised less in opposition to globalization than rather being integral to new forms of globalization (Adamson 2010). I will also suggest the central role of heritage and design in making certain kinds of dwelling (entwined urban and rural) both possible and meaningful in the Global South (Gupta 2018b). These new sustainable lifestyle formations are taking place the world over as a result of the increasing congestion, high rates of pollution, and difficulties of living in global city spaces that are increasingly becoming nondescript 'non-places of supermodernity' (Augé 1995), where one is anywhere and nowhere at the same time and mobility is restricted due to the overpopulation of people and things (cars in particular). These conditions of urban living have of course been worsened by the global coronavirus pandemic (2020–). Instead, and even more so now, there is an active return to history and culture, in search of alternative forms of the 'good life' (Ahmed 2010; Appadurai 2013; Fisher 2014) in global hinterland pockets the world over. They, in turn, promote an ease of mobility within localized spaces, by way of innovative features that restore, revive, and repurpose heritage through careful and clever design (Jackson 2014; Gupta 2019d). In a sense, I am proposing an ethnography of heritage futures (Clammer 2012) and (smaller) community-based heritage building through a theory and method of design, two aspects that I take up in my conclusion. Lastly, it is my long-term engagement with Goa that has also placed me in a unique position to foreground a specific case study of heritage and design for this new Cambridge Elements Series on Critical Heritage Studies.

1.2 Hinterland Goa

I have been visiting Goa over a period of twenty-five years and have an intimate sense of this dynamic space that holds such meaning and continued curiosity for me. It is where I first conducted fieldwork during the summer of 1994 as a PhD student in anthropology studying in the USA, and it is the site on which I have built the foundation of my scholarly academic career, including the publication of numerous articles (on a range of topics including tourism and heritage) and two single-authored monographs (Gupta 2014b; Gupta 2019c). It is a fascinating and enduring relationship with a place that has taken on a life of its own, autobiographical aspects and ethnographic encounters that I elaborate on more fully in Section 2, 'Goa Dreaming'.

In other words, it is my range of research interests on the topic of Goa that has positioned me to write carefully about the politics of its past as a history of the present. First, it is one very much attuned to the ways in which Goa's Portuguese colonial past (relational to the historic role of the British in India) continues to sustain its idea of historical and cultural 'difference' (Trichur 2000; Gupta 2014a) from the rest of (British) India while still being part of it. I have written about how the state of Goa operates as an 'internal exotic' of sorts by way of its colonial difference (Gupta 2009b), a characterization that post-colonial India relies on to sustain itself as a geopolitical entity. This includes its forced integration into the Indian nation-state in 1961, a still-contested moment in Goa's decolonization process (Gupta 2019c). Secondly, I have shown how Goa's colonial difference got mapped onto its tourist representations and continues to feed both international and domestic tourism, a sector of Goa's economy upon which it is wholly dependent. As well, there is a much longer history of varied forms of tourism that Goa has experienced in the space left over by Portuguese colonialism: early 1960s European spiritual hippie tourism, Catholic religious tourism, trance music, package tourism (British and Russian mostly), and finally domestic honeymooner tourism (Trichur 2000; Newman 2001; Saldanha 2007; Gupta 2014a). Thirdly, tourism and heritage continue to overlap in complex ways (Kirshenblatt-Gimblett 1998) in the case of Goa and are very much tied to international, national, and local heritage politics, including donor funding and the neat packaging of heritage for tourism consumption. Velha Goa (Old Goa), the historic centre of the Jesuit missions and the resting place of St Francis Xavier's corpse, was put on the coveted UNESCO list of world heritage sites as early as 1986; it is an important site for Roman Catholic and Indian Christian pilgrimage and continues to play a vital role in Goa's heritage landscape. There is also a select envisioning taking place with regard to Goa's Catholic heritage; it dominates in tourist discourses even as Goa's Hindu heritage is equally vibrant and is being heritagized in interesting and important ways locally. Both are simultaneously caught up in larger pan-Indian discourses of *Hindutva* that rely on and put pressure on Goa's historic, cultural, and religious difference once again. Fourthly, there exists a longue-durée history of Goans moving within an intra-colonial Portuguese world from the mid-nineteenth century onwards in search of improved livelihoods (to Mozambique, Angola, Macau, and Portugal), which continued in larger numbers during the tapered end of colonialism and integration into the Indian nation-state (1947–61) (Gupta 2019c); this in turn has made Goa into a heritage destination both for Goans living outside Goa but still on the Indian subcontinent and for its multiple far-flung diasporas (UK, Canada, East Africa, Australia). These four thematics of research and writing, or rather conceptual framings, have been integral in shaping some of the background thinking for this Element.

In 2013, during my sabbatical year from the University of the Witwatersrand in Johannesburg, South Africa, where I currently live and work, I returned to Goa with the tentative idea of looking at its contemporary heritage landscape. I spent five months living in North Goa with my family in order to get to know this familiar place that felt very different thirteen years later, from the perspective both of my own life journey and that of Goa. Once I stepped away from the sun, sand, and surf of *sossegado* (a Portuguese word that refers to the relaxed lifestyle Goans supposedly inherited from their colonizers) amid its coastal beaches, I began to see a vibrant Goa that is 'quietly making itself' in its hinterland, even as its long-standing history of hospitality is an integral part of its larger cultural sensibility (Bruner 2001).

I revisit the theme of Goa's villages located in the hinterland, less as tied to the distinctive history of the pre-Portuguese system of communally owned community properties (*comunidades*), although traces of that system still shape the layout and livelihoods of each of the 347 villages or Indo-Portuguese *aldeias* that make up Goa today (Powell 2011). Rather, I have chosen to research these places as first or second homes for a group of globalized citizens, including many Goans who have lived in other parts of India or abroad (for both shorter and longer stints) before returning to a much changed 'home', urban Indian transplants mostly from Mumbai and Delhi, and, finally, Westerners who are choosing alternative lifestyles in a multifaceted cosmopolitan India of today. I see it interestingly as a new form of 'orientation' that is taking place, which suggests a convergence of South and North and a loosening of directional markers across and within the subcontinent.

I interviewed many of these 'urban rural dwellers' – predicated on urban living prior to a return to an idealized vision of rurality in the hinterland – to get a sense of their attraction to this nestled place caught between city and country life, taking advantage of both. Perhaps it is a search for interiority (both spatially and psychically) in an increasingly fast-paced world. Many of these returnees and migrants are in search of an 'alternative cosmopolitanism' found by way of a return to the rural after experiencing the urban (Nandy 2007), choosing to live in Goa's hinterland, away from its congested tourist belt in North Goa but still close enough to benefit from its readily available amenities. These attractions include a fast internet connection, specialized commodity goods (including both local and imported products such as French cheeses and wines from France and nearby Pondicherry, a former French colonial pocket in India), Goan spicy chorizo and *caju feni* (the local moonshine), and pristine beaches, only a few hours' drive away. Goa's village interior spaces then function as both work (ground) and playground; it is a form of artisanal living, Indian style, but Goan by design.

It is also the way that I meet these globalized locals – at literary events, art shows, and openings, in bookshops, as friends of friends – and the sparse directions with no road signs but rather visual markers that are given to find each of their homes ('look for the church on the left', 'the bridge crossing', 'the second four-way stop', etc.), nestled deep in Goa's hinterland on a quiet lane or street that I would have easily overlooked had it not been for the scribbled map hastily drawn on a napkin at the end of a late night or the detailed directions sent via email prior to our visit. It is villages with names like Siolim, Aldona, Bastora, Moira, and Utorda that I sound out so as to become familiar with them as I try to look at a road map to locate the exact lane, driveway, house. However, these quiet changes both redefine and entangle village life with urbanity as much as they index a telling shift in the attitudes and orientations across North and South India and the West towards urban life itself. This initial research (over a five-month period in 2013) in some ways led me deeper into the labyrinth of Goan village life and caused me to undertake multiple follow-up fieldwork visits (between 2015 and 2019) in order to fill out this set of portraits of persons with certain long-term commitments to Goa – it includes a mix of Goans who have remained in Goa; Goans who have lived outside Goa (either in India or elsewhere) at some point in their lives; North Indian residents in Goa; and one Argentinian-Spaniard; all of them are busy redesigning Goa's heritage in very personalized and politicized ways.

Lastly, this Element is very much a reflection on Goa's dynamic heritage and design landscape, one that is about seeing a certain style of heterogeneity in order to think through the layering of different historical, cultural, spatial, and architectural representations, subjectivities, and mobilities over the longue durée. For the specific case of Goa, as caught up in 'in-between zones of civilization' (Feutchtwang and Rowlands 2019), it combines and adds design influences from the Portuguese, but also the Dutch, British, and Mughal, from Hinduism, Islam, and Catholicism, and is still in some sense ongoing as new micro-design ideas are adopted and adapted to fit Goa's changing heritage and lifestyle choices. Here, I argue for Goa's continuing ability to domesticate the world unto itself following Jeremy Prestholdt (2008). For me, this twinned conceptual framing of designing heritage and ethnography as design offers a potential entry point into the mood and texture of post-colonial Goa today, one that is framed by my own long-standing expertise and familiarity with Goa from both a scholarly and experiential standpoint.

1.3 Ten Acts of Portraiture

This introductory section has briefly outlined my conceptual framing of heritage and design as well as my long-term engagement with this place called Goa. I enter the 'heritage-scape' (Di Giovine 2009) that is Goa today by way of ethnography as a form of design to approach design. My ten portraits are equally of persons and things: of markets, cloth, books, architecture, photography, houses, food, and villages. They reveal Goa to be a site of layered histories and affects, of travel, mobility, and design innovation. Each heritage practitioner showcased here sometimes conforms to, endorses, or counters Goa's multiple representations, as well as contributing their own, one that is often tied to the biographical and in pursuit of Goa as a 'lifestyle', an alternative form of cosmopolitanism (Korpela 2013; Nandy 2007: vii). Ethnography as a form of design also serves as a fitting passageway into Goa's contemporary heritagization in the hinterland, following small lanes, gravel roads, and handwritten street signs to look for certain 'micro-narratives' of history, culture, and difference, all rooted in design. To conclude, I provide here a summary of the sections to follow (2–8), suggesting that my small Element offers up a series of portraits of a range of heritage makers, places, and projects based in Goa who are designing its heritage landscape for the twenty-first century. These acts of portraiture are descriptive, visual, lyrical, intimate, and painterly in their attempt to grasp the person's lifeworld of heritage and design.

Goa Dreaming: Section 2 sets up my own historical relationship and engagement with Goa the place through a series of encounters, visits, and experiences. It is an auto-ethnographic reflective piece that sets up my research on Goa's hinterland heritage and design landscape.

Market: Section 3 is a portrait of graphic designer Orijit Sen and his innovative 'Mapping Mapusa' project, run through Goa University. The Mapusa market is a historic colonial bazaar that is still very much in use by locals and foreigners alike and which includes generations of traders selling a range of Goan intangible heritage food items (coconut-leaf baskets, Goan *pao* (bread), rock salt, prawns, and pork *sorpotel*, to name a few). I helped map its various sections and stalls (by way of photographs, videos, life histories, and drawings) with groups of Goan students over two short courses that took place in September and October 2013; participant observation in this design project will provide the basis for my analysis. I also look to its future iterations, as it is still ongoing and has developed a digital life of its own.

Cloth: Section 4 is a tale of two Goan tailors, the late Wendell Rodricks and Savio Jon, whom I interviewed first in 2013; I interviewed Savio again in 2019 alongside his fashion muse Sacha Mendes. Wendell and Savio are both products of a longer global history of Goan tailoring and diaspora making that I have written about elsewhere (Gupta 2016); each is turning cloth into a different heritage project for today, the former a fashion designer and author of a book on the history of Indo-Portuguese sartorial designs entitled *Moda Goa* (Rodricks 2012b) and the latter a fashion designer who relies on indigenous cloth and weaving practices to pattern dresses that are sold from his ancestral home in the village of Siolim. More recently, and before his untimely death in February 2020, Wendell had been involved in opening up Goa's first costume museum and research centre in his ancestral village of Colvale (forthcoming in late 2022). My section also includes a brief profile of Sacha Mendes as a heritage practitioner of cloth in her own right; she is the proud owner of an innovative shop that promotes local design; it is a space set up on the bottom floor of her family's home in Panjim, the capital city of Goa.

Book: I focus on two literary figures in Section 5. Diviya Kapur is a trained advocate and former Delhi resident who moved to Goa fifteen years ago, and Frederick Noronha is a Goan journalist; both keep the literary and scholarly alive in Goa today, the first by way of a bookshop called Literati that revives the book and a reading culture as heritage, and the second through the running of a small alternative academic press called Goa,1556 which solicits and publishes a range of books centred on Goan heritage, tangible and intangible. I have followed closely their respective innovative design projects over many years, both of which will provide the basis for my acts of portraiture.

Architecture: Section 6 is a portrait of Goan architect Gerard da Cunha, who has worked on various heritage museum projects, including the publication of a book dedicated to Goa's historic Indo-Portuguese styled houses (1999), the building of a small museum to house the research materials gathered together during the development of this same book project, his involvement in the recent restoration of the sixteenth-century Portuguese Reis Magos Fort, and lastly, the making of an archive and museum space to honour famed cartoonist Mario de Miranda's (1926–2011) illustrations of Goan life. I have interviewed Gerard multiple times over a period of ten years, and I write about his evolving design ideas for a set of diverse architectural projects.

Village: Section 7 is a portrait of Goa's villages, where I have lived and worked alongside many creative persons. I first focus on the villages of Saligao, Chikhli, and Moira, which I know intimately, having recently spent time living and experiencing daily village life in all three of them. The section is simultaneously a portrait of two Goa-based heritage practitioners and two locations, North and South Goa. Lola Mac Dougall is a Spanish curator and photography specialist, who has been living in North Goa for twelve years and who has fashioned Goa's architectural landscape (including its Indo-Portuguese Catholic churches, houses, and village interiors) as backdrops for her biannual photo festivals (February 2015 and November 2017), both of which I attended and was involved in setting up. Savia Viegas is a fiction writer and painter whose life journey returned her to Goa from Mumbai later in life and in an unexpected way. I spent time with the novelist and painter in her ancestral home in Carmona and gained a sense of how the village functions as the medium and canvas for her writing and visual projects.

Goa by Design: In Section 8, I return to Goa's dynamic heritage design landscape, gesturing to its future iterations as well as to the building of a heritage community of sorts in the hinterland where these ten practitioners are engaged, interacting and involved with one another's projects. I emphasize Goa's distinctive features as well as its sustainability as a design model *of* and *for* additional places and processes of heritagization, incorporating the old and new, and take into account history and culture. It also serves to revisit the theme of heritage and design, the topic that frames this Element.

AN INTERLUDE:
GOA DREAMING

Illustration by Orijit Sen, Goa. Copyright 2022.

2 An Interlude: Goa Dreaming

This Element is about my long-term engagement with a place called Goa. In this second section, I take the framing idea of portraiture in order to briefly sketch my own auto-ethnographic relationship to this dynamic space and its changing heritage and design landscape. It is an interlude, a space of memory, of what I call Goa dreaming (where past, present, and future collide), written one day while living inside Goa's hinterland, a reflective moment during my residency in the village of Chikhli, whence came my desire to write through a genealogy of sorts of my own anthropological encounters with this place over a twenty-five-year period.

I first visit Goa in June of 1994 from the USA to see if I want to spend the next ten years writing about this place for my PhD dissertation in cultural anthropology. I step down from the bus after an overnight trip from Mumbai, see the verdant rice paddy fields and sixteenth-century baroque architecture, and confirm to myself that yes, I do want to. I stay as a guest in the holiday home owned by my friend Meena's maternal uncle in the village of Candolim. She has graciously asked on my behalf, and he has extended an invitation. Back then, the sole marker for finding the Lakhanpal house was Bob's Inn, which is still in existence and very much a gathering place for long-term British expat residents. I have often passed by it on more recent visits to Goa, as it is a designated stop on the now much-trafficked coastal-belt tourist bus route. I always remember it as a signifier of my first visit to Goa. The oversized villa where I live for the duration of my stay is a funny place. Since the monsoon is in full swing during that Indian summer, it is empty save for the caretaker, Dr Cardoso, and myself. I am not sure why he is called doctor, but he just is. He serves me oversized plates of fish curry and rice for both lunch and dinner, so much so that I get sick of eating it and almost don't touch it for the next ten years of coming to Goa. I underestimate the power of the monsoon to shape my fieldwork; I am only able to go out in the afternoons when the rains clear for a bit and the coconuts have stopped falling from their laden trees. When I do step outside, there is always the fear that I will die a quick death from a coconut dropping on my head. I take my chances anyway and get an initial sense of Goa, the place and its people, on this first visit. I know I want to come back for more.

I have since continued to build a complex relationship with Goa, adding layers along the way even as it continues to surprise me in small moments. I come back to live in Goa for thirteen months from 1999 to 2000 in order to conduct archival and ethnographic research on the history of the Expositions of St Francis Xavier, a sixteenth-century Jesuit missionary turned saint who is still revered in Goa today. I first stay in South Goa with a friend for a few days at a small, quiet resort on the beach in the village of Cavelossim in order to acclimate myself. It is a favoured beach I will return to over my year-long stay, and the place where I will later pick up a ginger-coloured stray kitten, name him Luis (Cavelossim), and take him home with me. I move up the coast and inwards to rent a flat in a complex called 'Landscape City' in Alto Porvorim, a small stopover town between Panjim and its northern tourist beaches. It will be my home for the next twelve months. It is conveniently located near a major crossroads where I can catch a bus to elsewhere and within walking distance to the Xavier Centre of Historical Research (www.xchr.in). I spend my days conducting archival research and fieldwork in Old Goa, where the corpse of Xavier is housed inside the Church of Bom Jesus. There is no internet at home, and barely a grocery store within walking distance. I frequent the local STD (Subscriber Trunk Dialling) booth on Sunday afternoons to check in with my parents in the USA and stop by Mario's shop for basic goods. I befriend Rukshana, a Parsi-British graphic designer by training and busy working on the *Houses of Goa* book for architect Gerard da Cunha, who is featured in this book. Rukshana lives half the year in London, the other half in Goa. She introduces me to a whole world of interesting people living and working in Goa – Sangeeta and Rajesh, recent transplants to Goa from Delhi who are starting up a food court in Calangute; her sister Nazneen who had fallen in love with a Goan named Ricardo and moved here thereafter in 1994 to build a life together. I meet Rukshana's parents, who have decided to retire to Goa, buying up an old property in Candolim that will later become Café Chocolatti. I also start babysitting Naz's young daughter Rhea; they live nearby within walking distance of my flat in Porvorim. The three of us go together to Angel's Resort to use the pool off season. I would go to her home afterwards to sample the truffles that she was experimenting with, bringing back suitcases full of chocolate from visits to London to see her brother. My parents come for a first-time visit to Goa; it is their fortieth wedding anniversary, so I treat them to a weekend at the Taj Fort Aguada Resort and Spa in Candolim (www.tajhotels.com/en-in/taj/taj-fort-aguada-goa/). They love it, and I get a glimpse of a fancy Goa that I have not experienced before, of five-star hotels and high-end tourism.

My next visit takes place in December 2004, in order to attend a decennial Exposition of St Francis Xavier. I have successfully completed my PhD the year before. I want to visualize in the present what I have spent ten years researching and writing about (Gupta 2017). I also start thinking about the role of tourism and its effects (both good and bad) on Goan society, having purposely avoided it as a topic of scholarly research earlier on in my studies, as my interests lay elsewhere, in Portuguese colonialism and Jesuit missionary history. I have been careful to keep the distinction between being an anthropologist versus a tourist during my time living in Goa from 1999 to 2000, even as I realize now (following many anthropologists before me) that there is no clear divide (Crick 1989). My PhD research is eventually published as a book entitled *The Relic State: St. Francis Xavier and the Politics of Ritual in Portuguese India* (Gupta 2014c). I relocate to Johannesburg, South Africa to live and work (taking up a research post at the Wits Institute for Social and Economic Research at the University of the Witwatersrand) and move onto a different set of related research topics – the Indian Ocean, Mozambique, Portuguese decolonization, to name a few. The theme of Goa stays with me and makes its way into other writings; in particular, the topic of Goa's global diaspora in Mozambique and East Africa endures (2009a, 2014c, 2016). I find myself interviewing Goans who had followed a path of Indian Ocean circuits between Portuguese India and Portuguese Africa; their stories of migration as 'imperial citizens' (Metcalf 2007) will eventually become the topic of my second book (Gupta 2019c). I visit Goa once again in 2009, where I help to organize a small Indian Ocean workshop held at the newly opened Crown Goa Hotel in central Panjim (https://thecrowngoa.com/). Afterwards, I spend two weeks at the beach, renting a small flat with a South African colleague in a complex with a swimming pool. I am now finally ready to research and write about tourism, using my personal experiences as a tourist to shed light on what is happening in a changing Goa – my ethnography becomes a tale of waste and want, of Russians and British package tourists, of suitcases lined with frozen vodka, horny packs of Indian single men, and domestic honeymooners (Gupta 2014a).

In 2013, I come back to live in Goa for five months with my family during my sabbatical year from Wits University, with the tentative plan of studying its heritage landscape. I want them to see the Goa that I have come to know and love. Goa still exudes its charm despite the rampant tourism that has taken hold in the interim. This time around, we are living in the village of Candolim, a bit set off from the main coastal tourism belt and surrounded by rice paddy fields. We find a place to stay through my first friend in Goa, Rukshana, who owns a small one-bedroom flat. It is her cousin Kush who owns a larger two-bedroom flat available for rent on the fifth floor of this same building. I take long walks inland, avoiding the tourist belt but always passing by one of my favourite churches, Our Lady of Hope in Candolim. My family and I get used to and start to enjoy the rhythms of Goan village life – the *pao wallah* who comes by at 7 am without fail with freshly made bread, the local fish seller who hollers out at dusk as he rides through the village with the fresh catch of the day balanced precariously on the back of his bicycle, and the neighbourhood whitewashed church that rings every evening for 6 pm Catholic Mass. We three go on regular

visits to drink coffee and eat pastries at Café Chocolatti (http://whatsupgoa
.com/cafechocolatti), a restaurant that Rukshana's sister Nazneen has opened in
the interim. I befriend Diviya, who runs Literati and is profiled in Section 5.
I spend time with Alito Siqueira, a sociologist at Goa University whom I had
met in 2000 during my first fieldwork stint. He is avuncular and wise and pushes
me to pursue my burgeoning interest in developing a project on heritage and
design. He tells me to get in touch with Orijit Sen, who is teaching a short course
at Goa University and is profiled in Section 3.

My daughter attends a one-room schoolhouse in Saligao and has a teacher
named Lorraine, who had started 'Tiny Tots' after not finding a suitable daycare in
her home village for her own young children. We celebrate our daughter's second
birthday there with homemade cupcakes from a fancy French-styled bakery
located in the village of Siolim, named Patisserie Delicieux. We had hired an auto-
rickshaw for transport to and from school to home on a daily basis, but with the
full tourism season around the corner, our very polite driver Manav tells us in
mid-September that it is no longer worth his time to work for us, when he can
make big money driving international tourists around. We understand, for seasonal work is his bread and butter for the year. We rent a car to get around Goa;
I slowly get rid of my anxiety of driving in India and enjoy getting to know Goa's
back roads and smaller villages. We become friends with Lola and Nikhil, recent
transplants to Goa from Delhi. Their son and our daughter play together nicely.
This couple is just starting to think about buying an old property and settling in
Goa for good. Lola introduces me to the bakery near her house in the village of
Bastora. My love of all Goan breads starts then and there. We meet at Bhatti
Village restaurant in nearby Nerul for *rava* fried fish and Kingfisher beer. I start to
see a very different side to touristic Goa when I move inwards directly from a now
easily avoidable coast. I get to know a very different Goa this time around, located
in the hinterland. I see and feel that Goa has shifted its sense of self.

I visit Goa once again in February 2015, to attend and participate in GoaPhoto,
organized by Lola Mac Dougall, who is featured in Section 8. I return in
November 2017 to attend the second GoaPhoto, staying in the village of Saligao
where the event will take place. I rent a small cottage located on the premises of an
old Indo-Portuguese Goan house; Lola and I baptize it 'The Dollhouse' due to its
miniature size. Lola had found the place whilst scouting out potential sites for her
photography festival. It is perfectly located; I wander through this village that
I know well, looking for historic markers from the back of my mind. I find my
daughter's old daycare run by Lorraine, which has moved in the interim, down
a narrow alleyway that I have never noticed before, and discover a labyrinth of old
Goan houses. I walk to nearby Cantare in the evenings to listen to jazz music and
have a drink. I visit Diviya at Literati and pick up some new bookmarks that feature

Frida, her much-loved dog, who has since passed away. I ask after a book I have been wanting and end up buying instead a copy of Goa writer-in-residence Amitav Ghosh's most recent book, *The Great Derangement* (2016), which takes on the timely topic of climate change in the era of the Anthropocene. I meet Subhod Kerkar for the first time on this visit, seeing the signs for his Museum of Goa (MOG) all over Saligao (www.museumofgoa.com/), and go on a village heritage walk with him and a group of tourists, winding our way through the narrow back streets of Saligao and learning curious bits of its untold history. I befriend Frederick Noronha, who is profiled in Section 5 alongside Diviya Kapur; he had previously interviewed me for his online forum Goanet (http://goanet.org) about my book on St Francis Xavier. I return to Goa in 2018 for a two-week artist residency in the remote village of Chikhli and spend my time of contemplation thinking, writing, and walking inside Goa's heritage landscape (Gupta 2018b). I return once again to Goa in 2019 for two months, staying in the flat attached to Lola and Nikhil's newly built design house in the village of Moira. It is extremely hot and humid, for the monsoon winds are building up. I swim in their luxurious pool in the afternoons to cool myself down and meet them for drinks in the early evenings. I revisit old haunts and finish up my fieldwork and interviews, enjoying this precious time in Goa's hinterland. I start planning ahead for my next visit to take place in February 2020, timed for the inauguration of Wendell Rodricks's Moda Goa Museum and Research Centre (www.modagoamuseum.org/), not knowing that a global pandemic (and an untimely death) was just around the corner and would drastically change the whole world.

Illustration by Orijit Sen, Goa. Copyright 2022.

3 Market

My third section is a portrait of graphic designer Orijit Sen and his innovative 'Mapping Mapusa Market' project, run through Goa University. The Mapusa market is a twentieth-century colonial bazaar that is still very much in use by locals and foreigners alike and which includes generations of traders selling a range of Goan heritage items (coconut-leaf baskets, Goan *pao* (bread), rock salt, prawns, and pork *sorpatel*, to name a few). I helped map its various sections and stalls (by way of photographs, videos, life histories, and drawings) with groups of students over two short courses that took place in September and December 2013; participant observation in this design project will provide the basis for my ethnographic analysis. I also look to its future iterations, as it is still ongoing and has developed a digital life of its own through presentations at art festivals – Kochi Biennale in 2016 and 2018 (https://kochimuzirisbiennale.org/) and Serendipity in 2017 (www.serendipityartsfestival.com/). I conclude with a recent conversation and some reflections made by Orijit Sen at his design studio space in the village of Corjuem, Goa in May 2019.

3.1 Orijit Sen

I was first introduced to Orijit Sen in September 2013 by way of Alito Siqueira, a colleague and sociologist from Goa based at Goa University, who suggested that I get in touch with him. I was intrigued by Alito's description of Sen's new design project that he was developing as part of an initiative at Goa University to bring visiting scholars and artists to teach short courses over a three-year period. At the time, Sen was a Delhi-based graphic designer who had done commissioned mural work in Punjab, had founded People Tree (www .peopletreeonline.com), a design-based cooperative with branches throughout the country (including one in Goa in the village of Assagao), and produced India's first graphic novel, *River of Stories* (Kalpavriksh Press, 1994). He had also been visiting Goa since the mid-1990s, living there on and off for long stints over a twenty-year period with his wife and young daughter. Sen's short course is an attempt to use mapping as a form of design, as a way to get a sense of a marketplace set in North Goa, in the town of Mapusa. I sat down with Orijit on 21 September 2013 on the front verandah of his design shop and listened as he told me how he ended up doing what he does.[1] He had first visited Goa in 1984 and had felt connected to the place. It 'creatively inspired me', he says. He had trained at India's prestigious National Institute of Design (NID) in Ahmedabad, Gujarat, using his design skills to set up People Tree with his

---

[1] This chapter is based on interviews and ethnographic fieldwork conducted from August to December in 2013 and in May 2019 with Orijit Sen.

wife Gurpreet Sidhu (Gur for short) in Delhi in 1990; the impetus was to 'ideate' with skilled workers, creating a space where the workers would come up with their own design ideas, rather than him dictating to them what to design. It was his first attempt to set up a genuine space of collaboration between designer and labourer. He returned to Goa in 1998, to set up a branch of his then well-established People Tree Company in the village of Baga; it was first open all year, before he realized that seasonal businesses worked better in Goa, even as it was a short-lived enterprise (1998–2001). He still continued to spend time in Goa, for back in 1997 he had fallen in love with and bought an 'old fixer-upper', as he described it to me, in the village of Corjuem. He started screen-printing from his newly acquired property, selling his home-designed t-shirts to other vendors based in Goa. At the same time, he and his wife Gauri were raising a young daughter together, enjoying watching her grow up amidst the natural cycles and seasonal rhythms of Goan village life.

Orijit very much believes in the idea of 'thinking people who choose to live in Goa'; it is something that very much resonated with me when he said it. As his daughter grew older, he and his family returned to Delhi as their permanent base but still came back often to their village home in Corjuem, which at the time was still only accessible by ferry. Back in Delhi, he had paired up with restaurateur Satish Warrier, setting up Gun Powder, a restaurant specializing in South Indian cuisine, with a People Tree design shop next door in the trendy neighbourhood of Hauz Khas Village. They decided to have a go at the same successful collaboration set-up in Goa, which they opened in 2012 in a rented house in the village of Assagao, unsure if people would come, as they had not advertised it beforehand. Word of mouth worked, for the restaurant and shop were full on opening night, he tells me, as just about everyone in Goa knew about it. He had found a work–life balance, one that allowed him equal amounts of time in Goa and Delhi, to do his designing and thinking. Here the theme of living between two places, and design work as being shaped by these different experiences, is an important one and one that will resonate with other heritage makers profiled in this book.

3.2 Mapping a Market, Designing a Studio Space

When I first met with Orijit in 2013, he had only recently been offered the Mario Miranda Research chair (named after the famed Goan cartoonist featured in Section 6) at Goa University. He was excited about his prospective design project, which was centred on public art and giving back to the community, as well as the impetus for my own interest and involvement in his project as a teaching assistant. It was his love of markets, especially the Mapusa market, he tells me, which is how he came up with the idea of using it as the basis for the short course with Goa University. Orijit knows that particular market well, as he would go there for all his shopping whenever he was living in Goa. The idea of using mapping as a design element came from an earlier project wherein he had set up a bicycle outlet for rentals, handing out a cycling map of Goa with various routes, day trips, and so on that he had developed alongside. He then transferred this idea of mapping from bicycles to the Mapusa market. The idea was to explore the market from various perspectives, with the market becoming a 'studio space' for design work. The Mapusa market itself is an Indian market at its best and worst in some sense – a bewildering maze of stalls (after stalls) that I have experienced first-hand, selling everything under the sun, ripe with the smells of fresh seasonal mangoes, dried fish, hanging cuts of fresh meat, and row after row of women selling baskets full of freshly braided flower garlands. I had frequented the Mapusa market on occasion during my visits to Goa over a twenty-five-year period but did not know it well, except perhaps for its famed Friday markets which drew in a larger number of vendors and buyers on a weekly basis and which I tended to avoid for its crowds.

All that changed once I got involved as a teaching assistant for Orijit's first short course entitled 'Mapping Mapusa Market,' held over three weeks from mid-September to early October in 2013. There were a total of eleven students enrolled in this course, a mix of Goa University students and members of the public, and a range of ages, from twenty to forty-something. We first met one another on a Monday morning in front of the landmark statue and fountain of Hindu Goddess and mythic figure Shakuntala that forms the centrepiece of the historic Mapusa market (Fernandes 2012) and works as a common meeting place, and a form of orientation as well. As the course was set up over a three-week period, the first week consisted of simply getting to know the market itself, including its pathways and individual vendors through the act of walking, which works as an act of enunciation of embodied mapping. The point was to incorporate a form of 'sensory ethnography' (Howes 2004; Pink 2009), including it as a design element and as a method for feeling connected to the market. We started by walking and talking to vendors, noticing the smells and sounds of the market alongside which items individual vendors were selling. The students were also involved in creating an overall map of the market, which included conducting life histories, drawing sketches of vendors, and marking their stall numbers and locations on a larger paper grid that Orijit was busy compiling. Part of the larger project was to safeguard the market, for at various historical moments in time it had been 'under threat', either with vendors to be moved or with sections to be shut down completely by the Mapusa Municipal Council, the governing body that oversees the market's functioning and overall well-being.

Orijit's idea was to start collaborating with the vendors immediately, rather than leaving them external to the design process. He also set up a series of practical exercises in the initial days for the students to familiarize themselves with the space of the market. He sent one group of students to document five kinds of bananas available at the market and where they come from within Goa and India, and another group was tasked with finding out what can be bought for 100 rupees, items that best represent the market as producing both local, organic goods (such as jackfruit cakes) and global, foreign, and synthetic goods (for example, a Chinese-made guitar). The second week involved setting up individual and group projects with potential vendors. The idea was also to start thinking about mapping as a form of design. At one point, Orijit posed the question to all of us: 'Why are the flowers positioned next to the dried fish sellers?' His response confirmed the importance of design thinking: 'Perhaps it was a way to cover up the smell of the fish (with the flowers), a balancing act between practicalities and aesthetics'. The third week of the short course consisted of creating final group or individual projects that would be put on display at the closing exhibit, which was scheduled to take place in the covered section of the main entrance to the Mapusa market at the end of each of the two courses, in October and December, respectively.

Throughout the two sessions, I helped the students formulate their project themes, holding meetings with individuals and group members from the verandah of Orijit's People Tree shop in Assagao which served as our base to think and design. I also went along with Orijit to several meetings he had organized with the Mapusa Municipal Council, seeking both general advice on the functioning of the market more generally and permission to hold the final exhibit within the market space over a weekend. His idea was to make the event an interdisciplinary community arts project that revived the 'life and culture' of Mapusa and was 'delightful' (Orijit's words) not only to market shoppers but also to vendors.

The closing exhibition, held on a Saturday, 5 October 2013, was 'delightful' indeed, despite the pouring rain all day, a last unexpected monsoon shower to open the winter season. Orijit had enlisted the help of one of his employees from People Tree to design a marquee to advertise the event. I had helped do the summary write-ups for all the projects, which were to be mounted on the display board. There was a full crowd, including Alito Siqueira from Goa University and members of the Mapusa Municipality, alongside members of Goa's public, both vendors and consumers alike, who loitered throughout the day to learn about themselves and others, to laugh and smile as they recognized themselves in videos, drawings, and so on. Most of the student projects showcased at the final exhibition were thoughtfully executed and well designed, touching on various aspects of the marketplace. One pair of students focused on the Repair section (a dying trade of fixing umbrellas, lighters, sewing machines), producing a short film showcasing several of the vendors; another pair produced a series of drawings (an art manual of sorts) on all the medicinal plants on offer at the market. A third student working alone enacted a dramatization of price discrimination at the market (wherein I was asked to act out being the 'foreigner'), injecting a touch of humour in his play. A fourth student had positioned a time-lapse video camera in an upstairs window of a nearby hotel that overlooked the market and produced a fascinating view onto the daily activities of the market over a twenty-four-hour period that played on a loop as part of the final exhibition. All of these design projects incorporated innovative methodologies of tracing and mapping histories, persons, thematics, and layouts.

A few days after the exhibit opening, Orijit and I sat down to reflect on some of the initial findings from the first short course. Initially, he had been surprised by the lack of knowledge of the market beforehand on the part of the students. However, they also brought lots of 'vibrant energy and new ideas', and gave 100 per cent of themselves, without necessarily a larger end goal, he tells me. It was also important, he said, to think more about what skills versus technologies the students brought to the various projects they developed. Overall, he could see that the students felt connected to the market as a result of their projects, he tells me. It is a point that resonated with me, as I now had a mental map of the market, one that would serve me well during future visits. Without getting lost, I now knew where to locate my favourite things – dried squares cut from Alphonso mango, smoky sweet pinagr desserts, and butterfly-shaped fresh bread loaves. I also discovered a whole range of products (flip flops, leather chapals, paper, lace) that I would have not known about save for my involvement in this project. Throughout the design process, Orijit had the students create a booklet on the Mapusa market, which included a map detailing vendor sections, and with various properties and interpretations of the market put forward through brief biographies, photographs, and sketches of vendors, in order to make them come alive as people. It is mapping as storytelling for Orijit that I see happening.

Lastly, we reflected on the lessons learned and ways to develop the Mapping Mapusa project further for future iterations. His hope was to continue building up the project, to represent the market as an organic whole, with more resolution and detail as the art project builds, bringing in a range of other disciplines – sociology, art history, history, anthropology – and employing a range of presentation strategies – drawings, performance, video/film, photographs, and multimedia. In the meantime, Orijit started creating a Wordpress website (https://mappingmapusamarket.wordpress.com) that would archive all past and future events, including uploaded videos of life histories with vendors, teaching materials, drawings, blogs, final project exhibits, and so on, in order to keep the market alive and online as an active, changing studio space. Orijit was also interested in developing his own art designs, ones that would come directly out of the Mapping Mapusa Market project, and his personalized experiences with the market itself as a commercial and social space that counters globalized mall culture. Under Orijit's watchful eye, mapping takes on a variety of genres – as forms of storytelling (of life histories), spatial memory-making, and artwork – and functions as a new kind of multifaceted heritage tool that can be utilized for present and future community building.

3.3 Mental Mapping, Artwork, and Building a Residency

Six years later (May 2019), and I am in Goa again to catch up with Orijit and see how the life of the Mapping Mapusa design project has developed in the interim. I also find myself visiting the Mapusa market frequently, as I am staying close by in the village of Moira. My mental spatial map of the market remains intact from earlier, and I find everything I need to set up house and more. I realize how much I know and enjoy this market, based largely on my familiarity with the vendors – their names and faces, shops, and rich life histories. I phone Orijit, and we agree to meet at his village home in Corjuem. As usual, I get lost trying to find his house, which is located down a small but majestic long, narrow alleyway in the heart of the village, but eventually I see his now familiar long hair and slight stoop as he comes out to greet me. I also meet his wife Gauri at long last. A lot has happened in the interim, and in unexpected ways. Over tea, I learn about his involvement as a guest artist at the Kochi Biennale in 2016 (https://kochimuzirisbiennale.org/), and the Serendipity Arts Festival in 2017 (www.serendipityartsfestival.com/), an arts festival that takes place in Goa on an annual basis. He shows me images from his laptop, of the artwork he presented at these prestigious art-exhibition spaces based on an accumulation of three years of notes, drawings, and teachings for the Mapping Mapusa Market course (2013–15).

For the Kochi Biennale in 2016, he presented three distinct works (on Punjab, Hyderabad, and Mapusa) using the common theme of 'Art as Play'. He shows me a video online from the Biennale, and I see a group of young people laughing and smiling as they put together oversized puzzle pieces laid out on a table that fit together to create a mural image of a scene from the old city of Hyderabad. For his Mapusa art exhibit, Orijit tells me that he created large-scale profile images of many of the female flower sellers and added a few fictional ones into the mix. He created a staged version of the Mapusa market, with people having to walk through the alleyways of the portraits of the flower sellers and ask questions based on the bubble dialogues he had created. Participants needed to consult a map in order to answer five questions from the fifty available; it served as a way of orientation, of creative learning, and mental mapping of the market. It was a 'map-cum-comic-cum-game' interactive art project, he tells me; and it was very popular with the audiences, for many came back to try again in the hope of winning a prized print designed by Orijit from the Mapping Mapusa Market project.

For the Serendipity Arts Festival held from 15–22 December 2017 in Goa, he followed a slightly different format and drew out scenes from the Mapusa market in large scale (twelve different panels) alongside bubble conversations between vendors and buyers, creating a virtual treasure hunt in the process. He watched as visitors from Goa recognized themselves and found clues in the images and conversations on the walls surrounding them as they walked through the Adil Shah Palace in Panjim, a heritage building that had been recently transformed into an art space for Serendipity by Goa-based architect Gerard da Cunha, who is profiled in Section 6. Throughout these realized art projects based on Sen's design interventions with a specific market, themes that came up during the short courses that I was involved in also appeared again, those of engaging with a place (what makes a place a place), art as play, and a questioning of the (high) art world, and finally, the idea of what constitutes art. These themes were all central to Orijit's large-scale art installations that he produced based on the Mapping Mapusa Market project.

I also learn about the recent Christian Dior controversy that Orijit had been involved in, and the financial windfall from it that has enabled him to realize his dream of fixing up his Corjuem house and turning it into an artist residency. A January 2018 cover image on *Elle India* magazine had featured Bollywood actress Sonam Kapoor in a French Dior designer kurta-styled dress made of red cotton featuring a yoga block-print detail. It was Orijit's now grown daughter Pakhi who first saw the cover photograph and noticed the similarity of the print of the Dior dress with one that Orijit had designed years earlier for People Tree and which featured a seated figure in a lotus yoga position. Orijit sued Dior for copying his design and won his case of plagiarism, an outcome that surprised many in the global fashion industry. An out-of-court settlement was reached, and an undisclosed amount of money was given to Orijit. He also issued a statement to the press, saying 'I'd like to set an example here, so these mega brands with mega budgets think twice before plagiarising the work of small independent creators with impunity' (www.scroll.in/latest/880649/french-brand-christian-dior-settles-plagiarism-dispute-with-indian-design-studio-people-tree).

This unexpected payout came at a good time, Orijit tells me, as it enabled him to move full time to Goa in the past year, living with his wife in a small side cottage while he dedicated himself fully to renovating and expanding his village house into a functioning artist residency. He hired an architect who conducted what he described as a 'gritty assessment' of what needed to be done. He has big plans, I can see, as he takes me on a guided tour of the large plot of land featuring a sweeping verandah that looks onto a large front garden full of trees and a back area with spaces for future pottery and woodworking studios. It will be a slow organic process to complete the work on the house; Orijit estimates about two years in total. He wants to retain the essential characteristics of the house, including its Goan heritage oyster-shell windowpanes, while taking into account how the house behaves during the seasons, especially during the heavy monsoon rains. He is taking note of the leaks and the creaks in the house in the meantime. He started dreaming about every window and door so that he now has it all mapped out in his head, he tells me with a grin on his face. It will either be called 'People Tree Studio', the name he had given it back in 1997 when he purchased the plot of land, or he will change it back to 'Blessing', the original name given to the house by its original owners, as it is a fitting one – it was a blessing from Dior, he jokes, that allowed him to realize his dream project. Orijit is busy 'ideating', you can feel it in the way he speaks about all the grand plans in his head. The Corjuem village home will not only be an artist residency, but also a multidisciplinary art space, including a mentorship programme for young people (for which he hopes to get sponsorship) and a communal living space for all the artists in residence. I easily envision all of these things happening in the near future and look forward to my next visit to Goa.

3.4 Digital Lifeworlds

After our meeting, I return to my village home of Moira where I am staying for the month, my head filled with Orijit's exciting plans. I go online to find an extremely articulate Orijit Sen describing his approach to art and the design incentives behind the successful Mapping Mapusa Market project. I find that this graphic designer has an impressive digital presence, offering a fully fleshed-out portrait of himself. I locate soundbite descriptions, phrases that sound familiar from our past conversations but were not available in such a concrete and polished language back in 2013 when Orijit had first started the project and when I had just come onboard (https://kochimuzirisbiennale.org/lets-talk-with-orijit-sen/).

I check out the Mapping Mapusa Market Wordpress site (https://mapping-mapusamarket.wordpress.com) and find an updated user-friendly website that includes meticulously archived short courses from 2013 to 2014, links to uploaded videos and interviews with Mapusa vendors, blurbs and blogs and insights, ethnographic-style descriptions of encounters, experiences, and so on, in and around the market. It is informative, fun(ny), simple in its design but still clever, a style I have come to associate with Orijit himself. His Wordpress site and digital portrait perfectly sum up the creative and critical design that underwrites this innovative heritage project, which takes a Goan outdoor market as its design object but also links it to larger global movements towards a renewed return to local produce, craft, and organic goods in the face of rampant consumerism and the emergence of malls and supermarket culture. I too would say that Orijit Sen's Mapping Mapusa Market project is 'splendidly graphic' (www.heraldgoa.in/Cafe/Mapusa-market-Splendidly-graphic/124151 .html).

What endures with Orijit's innovative project is that visual mapping of a heritage site both becomes a form of memory-making and storytelling and works to memorize, memorialize, and heritagize it for future generations of Goans who want to resist a globalized mall culture and will instead continue to frequent the Mapusa market in search of a range of local (already organic) and imported goods and produce. It is also a way of giving back to the people of Mapusa and the cast of characters (of vendors and buyers) that make this particular place such a lively and sustaining presence, for they very much see themselves in the student projects, his artworks, and lively Wordpress site, with the latter also functioning as a supplementary design studio. In addition, my ethnography of Orijit's design project works in tandem with his innovative ideas on mapping and tracing (mental, physical, online, and through artwork) to showcase an improved multimodal methodology, one that can potentially open up new heritage processes and community-based projects.

CLOTH/ING

Illustration by Orijit Sen, Goa. Copyright 2022.

4 Cloth/ing

My fourth section is a tale of two Goan tailors, Wendell Rodricks and Savio Jon, whom I interviewed in 2013 to 2014, and the latter again in 2019. Mentor and student respectively, they are both products of a longer threaded history of Goan tailoring, identity-making, and diaspora formation (Frenz 2014; Gupta 2019b). As Goan Catholics stayed at home or moved elsewhere, they took advantage of the everyday Western skills they learned from their Portuguese colonizers and transformed them into highly prized professions, specifically cooking, tailoring, and photography. As I have suggested elsewhere, these 'civilizing traits' became their signature markers of modernity that crossed the Indian Ocean with them as 'imperial citizens' (Metcalf 2007) and which they relied on to find or create pockets of work in places such as British India and British East Africa, where such training and skills (and in particular tailoring Western dress for white settler-colonial populations) were in high demand (Gupta 2016; Gupta 2019b).

Wendell and Savio are each turning the Goan heritage object of cloth into different design projects for today. Wendell has been designing Goa into his clothes since the 1980s and created the first line of resort wear for India. He has also focused on the history of Goan clothing, authoring a book on the history of Indo-Portuguese sartorial designs entitled *Moda Goa: History and Style* (Rodricks 2012b), and has been involved in establishing Goa's first costume museum in his ancestral village of Colvale, to be opened in late 2022.[2] Savio undertook an internship with Wendell early on in his career, before establishing his own label. He is a clothing designer with a 'quirky Goan take on fashion' (Wendell describing Savio in Rodricks 2012a: 213), one that relies exclusively on a range of Indian cottons and natural dyes. Savio designs his dress collection from his ancestral home in the village of Siolim for a steady clientele based largely in Delhi and Mumbai. He also sells his fashion line by way of close friend and muse Sacha Mendes, and her specialty shop in Panjim; she will also feature in this chapter for her parallel approach to Goan heritage, design, and cloth(ing).

---

[2] Interview with Wendell Rodricks, 23 November 2013. Very tragically, Wendell passed away during the writing of this book, on 12 February 2020. His untimely death prevented a second interview with him that I had planned for in 2020 and of course postponed the opening of his Moda Goa Museum and Research Centre: www.wendellrodricks.com/i/moda-goa-museum-research-centre. The enduring Covid pandemic has also been a factor in the continued delay of the opening of his museum, which is provisionally scheduled for late 2022, according to the above website. I dedicate this section to him.

4.1 Wendell Rodricks

Goa is like a house where lots of people are coming through.
(Interview with Wendell Rodricks, 2013)

I arrive on the doorstep of Wendell Rodricks' home 'Casa Dona Maria' in the Goan village of Colvale on 25 November 2013. I had emailed him earlier, and he had agreed to a one-hour interview starting at 11 am, with a formal sit-down lunch to follow. Prior to our meeting, I had been reading up on and researching Wendell and could see he was a very busy man about town, involved in a range of projects tied to cloth, heritage, and design. As we sat across from each other on his outside terrace overlooking the manicured garden, I recalled for him our first very brief meeting back in December 1999 at his second design space and boutique shop in Souza Towers – what he describes as his 'shop in the sky' (Rodricks 2012a: 207) – when I was in search of a New Year's Eve party dress for a fancy Millennium party I was to attend at Jimmy Gazdar's house in Aguada, North Goa. Even though he didn't remember the incident, he remembered the dress that I had fallen in love with for its daring design. As we talked about his life in fashion, parts of it sounded rehearsed, bits of biographical reflection that I had read in his recently published autobiography entitled *The Green Room*, appropriately named after the eponymous, makeshift behind-the-scenes space that accompanies any boutique show (Rodricks 2012a). However, by meeting him in person, I was also able to fill out my portrait of him, and gain a sense of his very real commitment to Goa, the place and its rich clothing design history.

Born in 1960, Wendell had grown up in Bombay (now Mumbai) as part of a large Goan expatriate community. He returned to the city of his birth after studying fashion design in Los Angeles and a brief stint of travelling and studying in France. However, after experiencing the Bombay riots of 1993, he decided it was time to search for a new home; and being gay and with a French partner made the decision easier, he tells me. He decided to return to his Goan roots, not knowing Goa very well but willing to give it a try. He was offered the opportunity to buy a family's 400-year-old ancestral property, located in his own family village of Colvale, which had come up for sale. He bought it with the intention of fixing up the house and garden before moving in. It was his fate of sorts, he tells one interviewer, with 'a dream leading to a house, a house leading to a book, a book leading to a museum' (www.nytimes.com/2019/03/30/fashion/museum-costume-goa-india.html).

Wendell tells me how Goa is culturally richer now than it was when he arrived, and that back then (in the late 1980s) there was only a small group of artists and designers in residence – including Remo, the well-known Goan musician and Mario Miranda, the Goan cartoonist who will feature in Section 6 and is part of the make-up of the Goan creative community portrayed in this book. Wendell also reminds me that there are many Goas – beach Goa, urban Goa, and rural Goa with its village lifestyle and artistic minds, a point that resonates with my own experiences of living in its hinterland. It was Goa itself that inspired him in his clothing designs and pushed his desire to put unknown Goa on the Indian and international fashion scene. He tells me how he found the right balance between urban and rural in Goa once he settled into village life in Colvale, and how it allowed him to live near nature and to develop what he hoped would be an eco-friendly clothing line that reflected Goa, with its incorporated ephemeral elements, like coconuts and shells, and its particular Indian ocean, wind, and sunlight. His intention was to create fashion that was as liveable as it was modern, he says. Wendell wanted to give India a sense of minimalism and bareness, a space that was exciting and felt good on the body, and light like a sea breeze. He was consciously putting Goa into his designs, for as he tells me, Goa gave a lot to him, and he wanted to change the way Goa was perceived from outside, on the larger fashion runway. He also wanted to link his clothes back to Goa's rich history of migration – including a more recent wave of writers, photographers, and fashionistas moving to Goa from the 1990s onwards – and continuing this same patterned design in his work. In a passage straight out of his autobiography, *The Green Room* (2012a) that echoes these same sentiments, Wendell writes:

Since my arrival in Goa, I had been stuck with the challenge of translating into my clothes the sea, breeze, the air of the *sussegado*. With *Clothing the Soul* [the name of his fashion line] I had finally accomplished it. There were three aesthetics of India which appealed to the international mind. The Royal ambience of the Maharajahs had held the fascination of travelers for centuries as foreign writers wrote glowingly about the elaborate costume and magnificent jewels in the famed palaces of Rajasthan and the imperial court of the great Mughals. As a result, garments in bright silks with embroidery had become representative of Indian clothing. In later years, Bollywood and colourful renditions of the Hindu gods created another Hippie-kitsch aesthetic. The third aesthetic that intrigued the Western mind was the Spiritual side of southern India, with its temples, yoga, Ayurveda, and so on. These aspects had not yet been translated into clothing – and I took up the challenge. Suddenly, the media was proclaiming me the guru of Indian Minimalism. And as I sent the sarong as an evening cocktail skirt and a sequined bikini top as a *sari choli*, I unconsciously gave India Resort wear as well! (2012a: 178)

Wendell opened his first boutique in late 1995 and named it 'The Wendell Rodricks Couture Salon' on Rua de Ourem in the heritage area of Fontainhas in Panjim. He reminisces about his first shop in *The Green Room*:

> With the river over the entrance to Panjim flowing gently by the row of old homes and new buildings, the setting was so picturesque that even after we left the shop, the owners retained the colours . . . .the shop was like a little jewel – warm, inviting, and with a great ambience. Even now, years later, I feel that it was a beautiful shop! (2012a: 186)

In a passage from this same autobiography that reflects on how much Goa itself has fashioned his designer sense, Wendell describes the opening of his first solo couture show in Goa, which took place on 10 July 1997. He writes:

> We planned the set, the ramp, the lighting, and the music. The Kala academy [in Panjim] had not done a show where the ramp flowed down to row K, right into the audience. The set was made by carpenters and painters from Colvale, and they were all invited to watch the show. I arranged for the clothes to appear in couture style. Each ensemble had a name. All of them were inspired by Goa and my own journey through life. The places we lived in – Colvale, Rue d'Alesia, Istanbul, Los Angeles – all featured as ensembles, as did Goan flowers, plants, birds, beaches, and abstract Goan concepts such as *passoi* (evening stroll). The clothes were sewn in Colvale and counted each day until the final forty ensembles made it to fitting. (2012a: 194)

Wendell is also well known for revitalizing a particular Goan heritage cloth, that of the Goan *kunbi* sari, the only sari found in the state of Goa. He set about learning how to reproduce the textured weave with its requisite red-and-white checkered design and ikat cloth worn by tribal Goan women, its production stopped under Portuguese colonial rule (2012b: 329–351, Chapter 21, 'Reviving the Goan Kunbi Sari'). He popularized it to the extent that Bollywood actress Lisa Ray and Sonia Gandhi, the Italian widow of former Prime Minister Rajiv Gandhi, were featured in popular fashion magazines wearing his designs (www.modagoamuseum.org). At a later point during our interview, Wendell tells me how he designed the Goan policemen's uniforms as a way to give back to Goa, the place that 'brought him back, and found him a home'. He also tells me more about the process of writing *The Green Room*, and how it started out as project with a small collective named the Goa Writers Group and turned into something bigger, which is as much an autobiography as it is a travelogue, with culinary experiments around taste and food, a sort of how-to manual for hopeful young designers. It is a style he also adopted for a later book on the taboo subject of Goan child house servants entitled *Poskem* (2017).

Meanwhile, Wendell was also busy with a second book project, an impressive tome that pays homage to Goa's rich heritage in cloth, costumes, and design. He weaves a historical and visual tapestry, one that showcases his skills as a researcher of Goan design history, an area that he started delving into quite by accident, when a well-known Goan journalist approached him to write a small article on the history of the *pano bhaju*, a traditional Indo-Portuguese dress worn by elite Goan Catholic women (Fernandes 2014). In a passage from his autobiography, Wendell writes:

> I was fascinated by the scholarly process involved in discovering the history of the *pano bhaju*. It turned into a passion. By the middle of the year [1999], I had decided that I would research not only the *pano bhaju*, but the entire history of Goan costume. It would, as it turned out, take eleven years of my life to write a book about it. (2012a: 211)

That book became the coffee-table-styled *Moda Goa: History and Style* (2012b) and shifted the perception of Wendell to being not only a skilled clothing designer but also now a son of Goan heritage. In a concluding passage in the introduction to his ode to Goan style, Wendell writes:

This book is a premier step to document, at a national and international level, the unique history of Goan costume. I have looked at events dispassionately, from a historical perspective. On a personal level, I must admit that Goans are what they are today due to the many peoples and cultures that have touched this land ... Despite our obvious identity with Hinduism, we learn how earlier faiths and tribal influences colour our clothing heritage. All these forces have brought us to the present day where Goa enjoys a distinct garment style, with an international aesthetic and an Indian emotion. Goan costume, a product of cultural and historical evolution, contributes to the themes of international design sweeping the modern world, where ethnicity is incorporated within the parameters of international wearability. Goans wear their clothing heritage with happiness, pride, and the consciousness of all that has passed before, and what will come in the future for Goan costume, dress, synthesis and style. (2012b: xvii, and for a critique see Fernandes 2014)

Wendell has produced a remarkable historically rich and highly stylized book on style (featuring glossy images by Goan photographer Mark Sequeira), one that is a mix of genres and spans time periods, from prehistoric Goa through to the second millennium, and which carefully balances both Hindu and Catholic early modern influences (including the shadow of the Inquisition) on the design history of Goan cloth and jewellery. It contains personal reflections, including the research journey itself that involved travelling within the state of Goa and internships abroad at Lisbon's National Museum of Costume and New York's

Fashion Institute of Technology (2012a: 218–234), and conversations with historians of dress and curators of costume museums, in Goa, India, and abroad. Wendell also tells stories around the archives visited, and the collecting of old Goan family photographs in full dress, etchings and drawings of old Goan costumes and distinctive styles worn by both men and women as markers of status. Lastly, the book includes found illustrations and drawings done by Wendell, some inspired during his research trips, as well as photographs from his own designer collections of the Wendell label over the years. In the end, the glossy high-quality production stands as testament and monument both to the design work undertaken and compiled by Wendell and to the rich heritage of Goan cloth and design.

The materials he gathered together for this vast project, researched over a ten-year period, would next become the motivation for and the start of the collection for his future Moda Goa Museum and Research Centre. Wendell spent the next eight years setting up the foundation and research centre, obtaining funds, setting up donor partnerships, and establishing a board of trustees to oversee matters. The idea was to house the new state-of-the-art centre in his village home of Colvale, whilst he and his French-born partner Jerome moved to a nearby rental property. Wendell, with his grand and ambitious design ideas to transform a Goan house into a museum, handed them over to Goan architect Arvind D'Souza to realize. These plans included creating a museum entrance, expanding the garden, adding height, volume, light, and temperature-control mechanisms to the main part of the house to protect the costumes, and finally building an archive library centre on the back of the property.[3] The opening of Moda Goa was initially scheduled to coincide with the opening of the Serendipity Arts Festival in Goa in December 2019. In a 2019 *New York Times* article that profiled the then-upcoming museum, journalist Sarah Khan writes:

> Mr. Rodricks and Mr. Marrel have amassed an 800 piece collection, ranging from a seventh century Apsara, or female spirit of the clouds and waters, found in a Colvale field where a Buddhist monastery once stood, to one of Mr. Rodrick's own successes: the Goan Kunbi sari, using a weave that had died out under Portuguese rule and he repopularized in 2011 ... When Moda Goa opens this winter [December 2019], it is to include a library and 16 galleries of exhibits tracing Goa's sartorial history from pre-Portuguese times to its current role as India's happy-go-lucky beach escape.
>
> (www.nytimes.com/2019/03/30/fashion/museum-costume-goa-india.html)

---

[3] I interviewed architect Arvind D'Souza on his plans for renovating the house into a museum and research center on 4 June 2019 at his architectural office space in Porvorim, Goa.

However, the initial December 2019 opening was postponed to early 2020 and then unforeseen circumstances took over – specifically, the tragedy of Wendell's untimely death in February 2020 – and delayed its auspicious opening. According to the Moda Goa Museum and Research Centre website (www .modagoamuseum.org), it is now scheduled for late 2022, which is still unlikely given the continued pandemic crisis the world over. Whenever its opening does take place, I do hope to be there in attendance, but sadly I cannot quite imagine it without Wendell there inaugurating the festivities with a bottle of French champagne.

4.2 An Interlude with Sacha Mendes

My conversations with Sacha Mendes over a six-year period provide an interlude (a breathing space, a journey with a slight detour) to arrive at my next section focused on clothing designer Savio Jon. It was Sacha (b. 1981) who first told me in 2013 that I should meet and talk with Savio, another clothing designer who had been quietly producing his own Goa-based fashion label and whose name I was not familiar with. I had come to know Sacha over various visits to her small design shop named appropriately Sacha's Shop in downtown Panjim;[4] it was a place that I loved going to, always finding some surprise item or gift to buy that was tied to Goa – its land, people, heritage – but also with a twist. And with each item (both old or new), she always had a fascinating story to tell, one that showcased its conception, production, history, and journey to her shop from her travels abroad and within India. Moreover, her personal style of dress always reflected that of her shop – casually beautiful, organic, creative, and carrying a free-spirited sense of self. I also enjoyed my conversations with her and learned over various visits her own Goa story, and how she comes from a big Goan diasporic family, with a mother who grew up in Kenya and Mendeses spread out in the USA, UK, and Brazil. Sacha studied Commerce (but always with a passion for clothing design) in Goa before leaving for Mumbai, where she worked for seven years in the fashion industry as an editor and stylist for various magazines, including *Elle* and *GQ*. She also took up sewing and pattern-cutting during this time outside of Goa.

In 2008, she returned home, feeling like it was time to come back, now with a full sense of appreciation of Goa and what it had on offer – including its precious people, fruits, flowers, and palm trees, she tells me. She also noticed immediately that more design work was starting to happen in Goa, projects that reflect Goa's heritage, creativity, and natural beauty. She feels the change, she

---

[4] Interview with Sacha Mendes at her shop, 18 December 18 2013, as well as various visits (and conversations) to her shop in 2015, 2017, 2018, and June 2019.

says. Sacha first started with a few pop-up shops selling things her designer friends made. In 2009, she took over the bottom floor of the 1938 house that had been built by her grandfather and which she grew up in, turning her father's old travel-agency space (after his retirement) into a creative design space. It is an intergenerational place, one where a range of local Goan designers are showcased, such as Savio Jon, alongside additional Indian couturiers she falls in love with during her travels, and it includes such items as clothes, handbags, and jewellery. For Sacha, her shop is less concerned with merchandising than it is about people's lives, crossings, intersections, journeys, and dreams. She likes to curate the space and picks and plans carefully, collaborating with designers to place 'what moves her' inside the shop, items she sources that reflect some sort of individual expression. It is less about buying than it is about an element of surprise for the customer and a sense of playfulness for her; it is about finding a new home for these favoured things even as retail in Goa is tricky, she tells me. 'Her shop is *her* response to Goa', in homage to a place called home, a gift of sorts to the openness and love of Goa she has in mind, akin to Prabuddha Dasgupta's photographs of Goa, one of which features Sacha and her parents Pamela and Rene Mendes at their home, located above the shop (Dasgupta 2009: 87). It was in this context that she mentioned Savio Jon as someone creative and like-minded, a close friend of hers whose clothing line she places in her shop, and a person I would enjoy a conversation with around Goan heritage, cloth, and design.

4.3 Savio Jon

Just as Wendell had described himself to me as a 'glorified tailor' during our interview, thus linking his profession to the longer history of Goan tailoring, a profession that travelled with many Goans on the move to elsewhere, Savio Jon too would consider himself a tailor, trained in the family profession. We meet for the first time, at the behest of Sacha, in January 2014 at his home in the Goan village of Siolim.[5] He narrates his life story to me over freshly squeezed carrot, beetroot, and pomegranate juice that he makes himself in his immaculate light-filled kitchen. Savio had grown up in Goa, born (in 1971) and raised on this same property, with a keen interest in fashion from an early age. He had learned to sew from both his tailor mother and tailor aunt and acquired his fashion sense from a father who worked overseas in the Middle East when he was very young and came home wearing the latest European trends in suits, shoes, and sunglasses. He recalls for me a 1980s memory of the travelling Goan tailor who would arrive at their house, carrying a sewing machine on his

---

[5] Interview with Savio Jon, 10 January 2014 in Siolim, Goa and 7 June 2019 in Panjim.

bicycle, and stitch up their clothes for the coming year, based on sketches and fabrics from the Middle East picked out earlier by his family members. Additional clothing designs and shoes would come from Portugal. All of these experiences shaped him and his quirky design sense; it is the small, unexpected details that surprise you, akin to the rocking horse I saw in his bathroom during my visit, its handles used to store toilet paper rolls. Largely self-taught, he was introduced to Wendell Rodricks in 1993 and interned with him for several years before starting his own designer label in 1997 (2012a: 185), fully taking over his ancestral property and fashioning it as a design studio-cum-art-gallery-cum-house, all in one, he tells me. During this time, he had stints of living abroad, in Europe mostly, and worked in styling on media campaigns and fashion shows over a fifteen-year period in order to support himself and refine his design sensibility.

His eponymous label Savio Jon (www.saviojon.com) is based on 'organic, pure Goan-ness' he tells me, even as his client base is mostly outside Goa, in Mumbai largely, and Delhi to a lesser extent. He chooses his fabrics carefully and uses only natural dyes to make what he describes as 'Deconstructed Western wear'. His designs are also a direct response to the resort wear that Goa design started out with in the mid-1990s, and for which Wendell, his mentor, had in a sense fashioned and created a global market. Instead, Savio's clothes are more tailored, with influences coming from London, Japan, and Belgium, and the music he heard growing up in Siolim (1980s pop including Madonna, Boy George, Cyndi Lauper, he tells me). His fashion sense is a return to his Goan roots but with a fresh take on them. Savio relies on organic cottons and muted colours to replace the synthetic materials, fussy lace, and bright colours of Goan fashion in the 1990s that were chosen by women because they were inexpensive and easy to wash and wear. Colour often signified formal fancy wear (as opposed to cotton which was seen as ordinary, not formal enough) required for Catholic church events. Savio likes that which is 'awk-ward', less highly publicized as compared to Indian fashion, which is largely Bollywood driven, he says. He believes that a long history of foreigners and Western dress in Goa has influenced and made an imprint on its heritage and design sense, thus making for a more tolerant space that allows for freedom of expression. And it is the number of outside photographers, models, writers, and architects now living in Goa that attests to that same artistic licence he feels in Goa and is most comfortable with as a living and breathing space. He wants to keep to that same vibe, with clothes incorporating those global influences just as much as they reflect lifestyle choices and weather patterns, a form of organic living and working. He is always asking where design is going, and purposely wants to keep his label small, even to stay unknown, he says, which is a very different way of thinking about design work and clothing design as compared to Wendell Rodricks.

We have a fun conversation about Savio redesigning the Goan widow black frock and revamping the polyester pencil skirt and blouse often worn by married Goan Catholic women as a sign of formal wear for church events. Both outfits, in some ways, still stand as markers of Goan Catholic heritage dressing. At the time of our first meeting in 2014, Savio had just completed a short stint abroad, having taken up a course in pattern-making for professionals at Central Saint Martins in London, a globally recognized fashion institution, to sharpen his tailoring and design skills. It is also always good to get out of Goa to get new design ideas and gain a fresh perspective on Goa, he tells me. In a published interview with *Elle* magazine in 2017, the author reveals a similar sense of personhood to the one I gathered in my conversation with him, as 'an anti-fashion fashion designer of sorts'. They write:

> Jon's love for fashion took hold of him early. At five, he was already thinking about clothes; at 12, he sat at a sewing machine and made outfits for his sister. Amongst his earliest inspirations was his father, who wore distinctly '70s-style safari suits and tailored trousers, the structured silhouettes influencing the young designer. Like many artists, often misunderstood, Jon grew up on the outside looking in. But that didn't bother or deter him. He flourished on the sidelines and came into his own. (http://elle.in/fashion/designer-savio-jon-interview/)

4.4 A Designer Duo

Fast-forward to 2019, and I am in Goa once again to follow up on my growing project on heritage and design. This time around, I am meeting Savio and Sacha together. Numerous emails later, we manage to find a time in the afternoon that works for all three of us at Sacha's Shop. It is 7 June 2019. I arrive early and have a look around, seeing some new designs that look and feel different from Savio's earlier collections (yet still admiring his clothing label), while Sacha's Shop retains that same charm that had drawn me to it six years earlier. We end up having our free-flowing joint conversation over cups of Indian chai on her front patio.

We do a round of quick catch-ups and overviews of what has happened over the past five years. I ask Savio if he has taken a break from clothing design, as a recent article I have read online suggests (http://elle.in/fashion/designer-savio-jon-interview/). He laughs and says he never stepped away, rather he works to his own rhythm, one that is tied to the seasonality of Goa and less to the larger fashion circuit. His clientele is the same – those who share his design aesthetics, he tells me. Savio has his hair drawn back into his signature ponytail and looks only slightly older, perhaps. He is wearing jeans, olive-green-coloured Birkenstocks, and a Japanese cloth jacket over a white t-shirt. I immediately see the influence of overseas travel, not only in the way is outfit is put together, but in the designer dresses I had admired earlier in Sacha's Shop, and which are also priced much higher this time around, a detail that also signals a different higher-end consumer market. He tells me about his recent visit to Japan for its Fashion Week (April 2018), and his falling in love with the 'simple lines' and 'organic cottons' that he saw on the runway. He travelled all over the country and organized a few pop-ups selling his designs. He came away from the trip with new tailoring ideas, he tells me, and with more of an interest now in the construction of clothes (seams, hems, details), but still with a focus on using natural fabrics. Since being back in Goa, he has been flirting with Dutch wax cotton, the textures of woven prints, raffia, and vintage buttons, he says, and is busy incorporating them into his womenswear line. He is avidly staying away from online fashion but has fully embraced 'fluidity, comfort, and casualness' instead; these sound to me like his new catchwords to describe his evolving style of fashion. He is still based in Siolim, still doing 'the whole Goa thing', a phrase he had used to describe himself in 2014 too. He has also started designing a line of jewellery that Sacha has just started putting out for display in her shop. Savio is now also selling his designer label here in Goa, and more in Delhi now, which in turn reflects a changing Goa and India, he says, one which puts more Western clothes on the fashion runway, and which has finally moved beyond Bollywood fashion to embrace something else, a temperament that is more ephemeral, laid-back, effortless, slowed down, and true to self, in the same way that Goa is, as much as it is a particular lifestyle that many aspire to in the design world.

Interviewing them together, I also learn more about Savio and Sacha's long-standing friendship that started over ten years ago (in late 2008) when they were both doing design work on Prabuddha Dasgupta's *Edge of Faith* photo book mentioned earlier as a design influence, Sacha modelling the clothes that Savio had brought along for the photo shoot. They reflect on their shared positionality in Goa, embodying Goan-ness, including its relaxed vibe, humidity, and hybridity, even as they both consider themselves insiders and outsiders in their home state. However, they can also easily shift away from it as a design aesthetic, in both similar and different ways, Sacha tells me. They are keen design collaborators and sounding boards for one another, one where a dinner party turns into an impromptu fashion shoot. Savio and Sacha had cemented their friendship over a trip they took together, travelling through Europe (Portugal, Italy, Brussels, Paris, Antwerp) by train and bus back in late 2014. They both still feel inspired by that trip, with so many design ideas for each of them coming out of it, based on a mood, a feeling, an energy, which they have incorporated into a clothing label and a shop, respectively.

I return to the author of the Elle magazine article, who seems to narrativize what Savio Jon is about, and what makes his clothing label distinctive. They write:

> Goa based designer Savio Jon recently made his return to Lakme Fashion Week after a 10 year hiatus. His S/S 2017 collection was every bit as inventive, thrilling yet totally laid back, as one has come to expect of anything Jon. Holland wax fabric patches, a dress fashioned from an electric green fishing net, and a deconstructed bandhani tunic with zipper details all walked straight out of his imagination onto the runway.
>
> (http://elle.in/fashion/designer-savio-jon-interview/)

The author pairs Savio and Sacha together in much the same way that I have in this section, asking 'who better to witness and trace his journey to fashion stardom –and now back to the runway – than Sacha Mendes, his muse, best friend, compulsive collaborator and proprietor of Goa's fashion fixture, Sacha's shop. Here, she talks to Jon about his new collection, life in the Sunshine State, and making grocery-bag couture' (http://elle.in/fashion/designer-savio-jon-interview/).

Meanwhile, Sacha has been caught up a few new exciting design projects of her own. Married now (since 2016), she and her husband Karthikeyan, a trained restaurateur and chef from Pondicherry, have decided to set up a new design space in the nearby village of Assagao. They have taken over an old house and are slowly transforming it into a second Sacha's Shop, which will carry over some of the same concepts of thinking small and experiences of slowness and careful curation of a Goa lifestyle that embody her Panjim shop. However, the shop will also be styled differently, with an 'alternate vibe and imprint' (her words), and will try to tell and share a different story. And her conversations with Savio have been integral to shaping the shop's future form and content, she tells me. It is a labour-of-love dream project for both her and Karthik, she says, as they will also move residence from Dona Paula in Panjim to Assagao village life in hinterland Goa. Sacha has been collecting treasures from their recent travels throughout India, and from Goa and Pondy more specifically, while Karthik has been perfecting his cooking skills to open a French Tamil fusion-style restaurant fittingly named Tamil Table inside their future design space (https://tamil-table.business.site/). I am invited to the opening launch, if it happens, she says, in a few months time, in July 2019. And if it doesn't happen then, it can't be rushed, so it will just happen eventually 'Goa style', she adds, with a smile.

Illustration by Orijit Sen, Goa. Copyright 2022.

5 Book

In this fifth section, I explore the 'book' as an object of heritage and design in Goa. I sketch a portrait of two heritage makers who keep the literary and the scholarly alive in Goa today. Diviya Kapur, a former advocate, does so by way of a bookshop called Literati that revives a reading culture and a love of books more generally. Frederick Noronha, a former journalist, does so by way of a small alternative academic press called Goa,1556 that he created, and which publishes short monographs on Goan history and culture. I have followed closely their innovative design projects over seven years, been involved in various aspects of them at different moments, and seen how they have grown and adapted, heritagizing the book – both the act of reading and the art of publishing – for a diverse Goan community, including its widespread diasporas.

5.1 Diviya Kapur

Diviya Kapur is an expert on books. She knows them, reads them voraciously, and is committed to promoting them at her bookshop that is tucked down a narrow alleyway off the main tourist strip in the village of Calangute in North Goa. Fittingly named Literati Bookshop and Café (www.literati-goa.com) and located in the front section of an old house with a charming verandah and garden, it has been a mainstay of the Goan literary scene for fifteen years. I had frequented her bookshop on occasion on earlier research visits to Goa (in 2005 and 2007), but I really only got to know Diviya when I was living in Goa during a five-month period in 2013. It was Literati that I would regularly go to with my young daughter to look for a new book to read. Her bookshelves were always expertly curated, with the latest fiction (and some non-fiction) written in English from Goa, India, and abroad on offer. She had at one point promoted Konkani-language fiction – which has its own prolific heritage industry throughout Goa and which I do not take up here – but as it did not appeal to her particular local and international mixed clientele, she went back to being a stockist of largely English-language books in print. She also had neatly organized scholarly sections on art, photography, sociology, and history tucked away in one corner of the bookshop. And Diviya was always on hand (as she lives in the back section of the building which houses the bookshop) to offer a recommendation or give a quick and insightful review of a book. Literati almost became a second home for us during this period. We would chat with Savia, her helpful assistant and right-hand woman who also enjoyed entertaining my daughter with the latest children's books on display, many of them from small independent presses based in Delhi. We would also regularly play with Frida, her dog (who would be featured later in life in a much-loved bookmark series produced by Diviya, which I still regularly rely on to mark my reading, despite their dog-eared appearance) and chat with Diviya about her most recent favourite read.

I also decide to help out with a mobile lending library that Diviya runs, one rainy monsoonal Saturday during the month of September 2013. Diviya's programme is named *Bebook*, which is the Konkani word for frog; she drives a van (freshly painted with a frog figure on it courtesy of our graphic-designer friend Rukshana, and its purchase funded by donations) around Goa two Saturdays per month, lending books and reading stories to children living in smaller, more remote villages where books are harder to come by. I see Diviya's commitment to this project as our motley crew (which includes Diviya, myself, my daughter, and a first-time volunteer by the name of Maria) makes its way from Calangute and drives an hour-and-a-half to the quiet village of Orlim, which is located beyond the city of Margao in South Goa. We park in front of the local Panchayat office and open up the back doors of the van, which has been converted into a small library, with shelf upon shelf loaded with books that are colour-coded (green, black, red, and blue) by reading level and age. Twenty village children suddenly show up out of nowhere, carrying the books they borrowed two weeks ago. Diviya is strict with all the kids; only if they return the allotted two books are they allowed to check out two more for another two-week lending cycle. A child shows up with a damaged book; she admonishes him and won't lend him another one. It is a hard lesson to be learned. She will let him resume his borrowing privileges next time around, however, she promises with a gentle smile. She also shows Maria the system of returning books and recording new loans, so that she can take over at some future date. I help with picking out books and handing them to the children, while my daughter has found a favourite book and is quietly turning its pages whilst she sits inside the van. We next drive to the nearby village of Benaulim and land up in front of the local Panchayat office. It turns out that a public reading inside the Panchayat building had earlier been planned, but it is now being used for a local meeting instead. Diviya quickly improvises and reads the story off her laptop on the porch steps, while the children gather around, listening and loving every minute of her performance. On the drive back to Calangute, we stop for a quick coffee and chat about the villages visited, the children she meets on her biweekly mobile-lending-library drives, and her love of books. It is this, she says, and the empowering act of reading (especially for children), which compels her and makes these literary adventures possible.

Four-and-a-half years later, I finally sit down with a very busy Diviya in February 2018 to hear her Goa story, and that of Literati, which is as much a tale of Goa and its migrants transplanted from elsewhere as it is of a businesswoman, her passion for books, and a shop.[6] Literati was launched in November 2005 with a reading by Isabel Santa Vaz, a Goan playwright; Diviya recalls the events for me over a cold beer, sitting on her side porch on a warm evening. She had spent a year looking for the right property to rent in Goa but was turned away either because she was neither Goan nor a white foreigner. She eventually gave up on the idea of a rental property and turned to friends in Delhi, who invested in her bookshop idea. They, along with her own savings, collectively bought the house that has become Literati. Before landing up in Goa, Diviya had worked in Delhi as a trained advocate for five-and-a-half years. Her family is from Bangalore, where she did all her schooling and also worked for eighteen months in the field of law before moving to Delhi. Most of her plans start out as small ideas that she builds over time, she tells me. And I can see that she is still pursuing all of them simultaneously, in some shape or form.

In 2008, Diviya had the idea to open a café in her outside garden space, which she did for a year, running it herself until she couldn't keep it going alongside the bookshop. She gave it up but now leases the garden to different restaurants during the day. At night, the garden becomes her space for book launches and for a movie club she launched in 2015, which she currently runs but barely has time for. She also tells me how she came up with *Bebook*, the mobile lending library that I had gone on tour with, four-and-a-half years earlier. It had a started out small, with her handing out donated books in boxes to village children, she says. She then bought the van, had it outfitted as a library, and registered *Bebook* as an independent NGO in 2013. She organizes an annual book fete on the premises of Literati to fundraise money and books and brings one group of village kids from her outreach programme to help her in hosting a huge jumble sale, with the proceeds going back into funding *Bebook*. She also has a loyal group of volunteers on hand to help out, many of them long-standing members of her book club, which she had also started a few years earlier. It was her way of avoiding going out with women, she tells me. All they ever talked about was their domestic workers or kids, two topics that were not of interest to her. Instead, it was books she was invested in, and the book club feeds that passion, with the monthly book meetings open to anyone from the Goan public. She selects books to read based on customer suggestions as well as what she can get hold of easily and inexpensively, with no scans or PDF copies allowed, she tells me. She purchases a minimum of fifteen copies, still believing in the material book itself as part of the reading experience. She then sells these copies to

---

[6] My profile of heritage practitioner Diviya Kapur is based on participant observation and conversations with her during my 2013 visit, including my trip in the mobile lending library on 7 September 2013 and a formal interview I conducted with Diviya Kapur at Literati on 19 February 2018.

book-club members, who in turn show up at Literati at the appointed hour, books in hand and open to an hour-long discussion. Afterwards, it is drinks and a potluck supper, she tells me. I attend one of her book-club meetings during this February visit and see a mixed group of young and old, Goan and non-Goan, a few Western long-term residents, but mostly a group of women laughing and talking about books in earnest.

Being in the book business is hard and always precarious, Diviya tells me. She is constantly doing market research on the latest global figures to assess the increasingly worrisome book situation. There are even times when she thinks she will not make it financially and will have to shut up shop, as everyone is both buying and reading fewer books, turning to Kindle and e-formats instead, or not reading at all. Interestingly, however, she has observed that the majority of the tourists on the beaches of Goa are still reading material books, a detail that helps confirm her enduring commitment to their valuation. Also, having famous writer Amitav Ghosh (www.amitav-ghosh.com) in residence part-time in Goa has also helped promote the idea of the book. Despite these hardships, she perseveres, and I see in these moments how much Diviya has designed Literati to be a centre *of* and *for* the book as a heritage object and a thriving reading culture (increasingly a form of heritage in itself, with this practice very much in global decline) in and for Goa, and one that comes out of her own love for it.

5.2 Frederick Noronha

Just as Diviya is committed to creating a specialized place where books and a reading culture are curated and revived, Frederick too is committed to the idea and object of the book in Goa, but from a different perspective. Over the years of visiting Goa (from 2007 onwards) and browsing shelves in various bookshops in and around Goa, I started noticing a series of small, slender books, with the neatly italicized press name Goa,1556 printed on the spine as if mirrored in water. These books always stood out and tended to be of interest to me, given my focus on a range of topics pertaining to Goa – biography, literature, anthropology, history, and art. I also appreciated the press's clever name, as the first Gutenberg printing press in all of India and Asia arrived in Goa via the Jesuits in the year 1556, fourteen years after the arrival of Basque missionary Francis Xavier in Goa to start up the Society of Jesus, a topic that I have written about extensively in my book, *The Relic State* (Gupta 2014b). In other words, the press's name immediately signals Goa's rich missionary and colonial history in print cultures and employs it as a way to continue the heritage practice of book-making and reading cultures, but at a very different historical moment and with a postcolonial public in mind, that is, for a Goa that 'needs a voice to articulate its own priorities' (www.goa1556.in/about-goa-1556/).

During my November 2017 visit to Goa, I started asking around and go in search of the person who had created this small independent press with its clever name. It was Diviya who told me where to find Frederick Noronha and that she had been impressed with his 'alternative publishing venture', as he advertised it on his website when he first started out. I was told to go to Saligao and look for Frederick Noronha's house, located very close to the four-way intersection that makes up the main bus stop in that village. Sure enough, I found his house easily enough and waited outside for him to show up, which he eventually did. A former full-time journalist turned part-time writer and book publisher, Frederick was in between meetings when I showed up without an appointment. Our visit was brief that time around. However, I did manage to get a quick look around his house-cum-office space and could see an extensive book collection on all things Goan, one that I would have to come back to explore in more detail.

It turns out that my second meeting with Frederick Noronha would only take place in 2019, and that was after many emails and phone-call attempts to set up an appointment beforehand. If anything, I found Frederick to be even busier than on my prior visit a year-and-a-half earlier in 2017. I persevered, and we finally set up a time to meet at his workspace in Saligao on a hot and humid late afternoon during the month of June.[7] Once Frederick realized that I was going to ask lots of questions, he relaxed and finally sat still, telling me his *Another Goa* story, which is also the title of his own book of essays (a mix of biographical and journalistic writings) published with Goa,1556 in 2009, and which pays homage to the place he calls home. We don't move over a two-hour period, talking non-stop as we sip iced tea. Interestingly, Frederick was born in São Paulo in Brazil in 1963 to Goan Catholic migrant parents. His father had been an engineer who grew up in Diu, another Portuguese enclave within India, and his mother was originally from Goa but had spent time working in Uganda as a nurse. Frederick grew up there until the age of two, before his parents decided to return to Goa after living in Brazil for ten years, an older brother in tow. His family history is much like that of Sacha profiled in Section 4, of a large global Goan diasporic family, with members living or spending time in Brazil, the USA, East Africa, India, and Goa itself. It is a story he is interested in telling at some future point, he says, as well as that of the larger history of Goans in Brazil, which remains largely unwritten.

---

[7] My profile of Frederick Noronha is based on an earlier visit to see him on 24 November 2017 and my 5 June 2019 interview with him in Saligao, Goa.

Growing up in Goa, Frederick was fortunate in that he received a good education, with good teachers. He loved books and the radio as a child – they were his 'window onto the world', he tells me. They both also shaped his career in journalism, which he took up at the age of nineteen, first as an intern at *O Heraldo*, a Goa-based formerly Portuguese-language newspaper which had just shifted to being English-based and was willing to hire non-elite Portuguese-speaking Goans like himself, he tells me. Frederick became Rico Fernandes, his *nom de plume*, as Frederick was too long for his byline. He was still completing his studies in commerce at Dempe College in Goa while he did his internship at *O Heraldo*. In the college library, he came across the published works of American anthropologist Robert Newman, whose 1980s reflections on the social and cultural transformations of Goa deeply affected him, such that he wrote him a letter and received a long response in return. Their correspondence turned into a long-time friendship between these two Goa specialists, one that still endures. More recently, Newman, now retired, compiled a two-volume set of books (a series of reflective essays on Goa over a fifty-year period) that was published with Goa,1556 (Newman 2019a; Newman 2019b); it was a way of giving back to Goa, the place and its people the subject of his forty-odd-year anthropological career.

After his graduation from college, Frederick worked in a bank for six months and hated it. He quit, even though it was considered a good job, in order to return to the field of journalism, working for *O Heraldo* as a full-time member of staff, as well as being the Goa-based correspondent for the *Deccan Herald* out of Bangalore. By 1994, he had turned to freelance journalism and has managed his career that way ever since. It suits him better, he says, to have his hands on a range of projects. During this time, he was also always dabbling in other areas of interest, taking up first an MA and then later in life, when he was in his fifties, a PhD in English literature at Goa University, which he is still in the process of completing. He also does some part-time lecturing in the same English department on the side and got married along the way. He has two children with his journalist wife, a Bombay Goan also named 'Pamela' like you, he says, only spelled with an 'e'. In a moment of reflection, he says that he doesn't love Goa as a place, but he understands it and is invested in it on a personal and political level. He finds Goa's history to be 'bizarre, fascinating and strange' but less than unique, a discourse that people use too often to describe Goa, and that he disagrees with. He strongly believes that the idea of Goa's exceptionalism blunts larger comparisons with other places in the world.

For Frederick, it is the right to information that is a game-changer, and that Goa's history under Portuguese colonialism and strict censorship has left many Goans without the resources to have access to information. He wants to see change happen and to open up Goa to that change. He believes strongly in discourses of the public, something that he first became committed to as a journalist. For Frederick, it is a fundamental right to free software that is shareable, a right to low-cost books, and a right to a Creative Commons for everyone. His 'motto' is to build and share, and it is that which will take a society like Goa's forward, where it will then produce its own knowledge. Frederick is very much a man of his word, for he was instrumental in expanding GoaNet twenty-five years ago (www.goanet.org/), an online global forum for all things Goan started up by a Goan Kenyan named Herman Meneses who was studying in the US in 1994, which has been indispensable to researchers like myself since its inception.

It is this same discourse on rights that has very much shaped Frederick's approach to starting up the small independent press Goa,1556. He had attended a course on publishing back in 2005, which sparked his interest, he tells me. The programme had been sponsored by the India National Book Trust, a government-sponsored organization that runs similar courses throughout the Indian subcontinent to promote independent book publishing. His course took place over an intensive fifteen days. Frederick found it incredibly useful, for he learned the basics of publishing (including its commercial aspects) and realized that that he could do a lot with very little. He began conceptualizing his own press along similar lines, committed to the idea that publishing the right way can become sustainable. By 2007, he had come up with the name of Goa,1556 and set up production on a small scale in a spare basement room of his house-cum-office. He asked a designer friend named Bina Naik to design the covers for free – Goa's 'cover girl' he likes to joke. She is indispensable to his publishing enterprise, for according to Frederick, she understands Goa's sensibilities and gets the cover right each and every time. The only difference is that now he pays her to do the important work she does. He tested the publishing waters with a first book written by his neighbour Yvonne Vaz Ezdani in Saligao, entitled *Songs of the Survivors* (2007), which took on the topic of the Goan community in Burma. He used a local printer to produce a run of twenty books, which he placed at Broadway Book Centre, Goa's largest bookseller outlet. With Ezdani's book selling out its first run and its profits put back into the press's coffers, Frederic realized that he had found a publishing model that worked.

Thereafter, Frederick began to solicit manuscripts from fellow Goan writers, and made Goa,1556 into a trust, keeping printing and production costs pur-posely very low in order to make the pricing affordable and accessible to a Goan reading public. According to Frederick, 'almost everyone has a book fighting to emerge: if you have a good story, and the persistence to tell it' (www.goa1556.in/about-goa-1556/). Goa,1556 quickly took off and found a place, filling in a missing niche in the literary and cultural space of Goa. He can't keep up now, he tells me, with the number of interested authors with potential manuscripts far exceeding his own ability to turn them into publishable books, with one new book published every few months on average and priced typically under 200 rupees (www.goa1556.in/about-goa-1556/). Frederick tells me that these authors are increasingly located outside Goa, but still writing on Goana-related themes. The priority is to publish Goan non-fiction books 'that shed interesting new light on various aspects that help us understand better this complex region called Goa' (www.goa1556.in/about-goa-1556/), along with a commitment to 'copyleft' wherein the author retains the copyright to the printed material, which is released as a limited edition as well (www.goa1556.in/about-goa-1556/). Frederick hands me an impressive-looking glossy catalogue with 140 illustrated book covers. The topics cover a surprising range on all things Goan, and include personal memoirs, village histories, Goan cuisine and recipes, Goan flora and fauna, gardening books, object biographies (the Goan coconut for example is featured in one book), children's fiction, Portuguese language and grammar guidebooks, Christianity and Catholicism, short stories, global Goan diaspora family histories, theatre, poetry, reprints of scholarly works that are currently out of print, and the list goes on.

Frederick doesn't seem surprised by the success of Goa,1556 but maybe it makes sense precisely because he credits Goa's vast diaspora in making Goa into a place, with Goa always already diasporic. Moreover, it is this Goan diasporic way of living and thinking that his press has tapped into, creating a vibrant writing and reading community as a result. Perhaps the flourishing of Goa,1556 is a fitting tribute to Frederick himself; he had mentioned earlier on in our interview that since he is has already once been an immigrant to Goa, he has no desire to be an immigrant again, and is content where he is, giving back to the place he very much considers home. Frederick still does all the proofreading and editing himself. It is a task he would like to delegate to someone else, only he can't afford to pay them a real salary, so he does it. He also realizes the importance of a good editor in turning a manuscript into a good book, so it has to be right person as well. For now, Goa,1556 is mostly a one-man show, and an impressive one at that. I ask him how I can go about reprinting my Goa monograph on St Francis Xavier with his press. He tells me to put him in touch with my editor at Manchester University Press, and he will try to secure the publishing rights for a limited second edition.

Frederick has many ambitious future plans. He is hoping that, in the next few years, he can hand the publishing reigns over to a person, or preferably, an institution like the Xavier Centre of Historical Research (www.xchr.in), a Jesuit institution that I know well, for it is where I conducted my dissertation research from April 1999 to May 2000. I think it is an excellent idea, I tell him. In the meantime, Frederick has various projects that he wants to see to completion. Two are his immediate focus: his unwritten book on the Goans of Brazil, and the completion of his PhD in the Department of English at Goa University on a topic that comes directly out of running Goa,1556 – that of the history of print cultures in twentieth-century Goa. Additional projects include editing a book on Goan media experiences and writing an alternative guide for tourists interesting in seeing a different Goa beyond its beach culture.

Even as Frederick looks ahead to all of these projects coming to fruition, he also can't help but get involved, make things happen in the moment, when he sees the immediacy of taking on a project tied to his love of books and reading. In 2018, he inadvertently found himself starting up a children's book collection, first buying a stack of them that he happened to come across on sale at Literati's annual book-buying fete. When Diviya found out what he was doing with these books, she offered them to Frederick for less than the normal price of twenty rupees each. He started accumulating more children's books, buying boxes and boxes of used books from larger bookshops in and around Goa for 400 to 500 rupees each. He also realized that there was a plethora of children's books available in Goa, and that many people were willing to donate them to his growing collection. He then cleaned out an old storage space in his Goa,1556 press office and turned it into a small lending library for the children of his village Saligao. That he happens to live next door to one of the largest public schools in Goa, the Lourdes Convent School, also helps. On average he has about twenty to forty kids traipsing in after school to borrow a book or two from him. He enjoys it despite the fact that many of his books are never returned. It would help with his accounting if he could register all the books he has, but that is a project for another day. 'A better read village would be a more efficient village', he says to me. This children's library project, alongside his innovative Goa,1556 press initiative, is yet another way of designing and affirming the book and a reading culture as a Goan heritage object. It is also about giving back to Goa, in much the same way that Diviya does with Literati and her mobile lending library *Bebook*. Finally, it is about promoting a right-to-information stance that is characteristically Frederick Noronha.

After our two-hour conversation, I walk back to the main four-way stop in the centre of Saligao and catch the local bus to return to the village of Moira, where I am staying during this visit in 2019. I decide to check out Goa,1556's website and find an online Frederick who is accessible and who is more willing to promote his big little press. He writes:

Launched on a rainy day (June 20, 2007) Goa,1556 is a quest to do things differently, and with goals that are different. Our aim is to democratise the production of knowledge. In our own small, alternative way. And we strive for quality simply by laying down high standards, while actively pursuing the goal of creating spaces for 'other voices' to be heard. (www.goa1556.in/about-goa-1556/)

I would like to suggest by way of a conclusion, that Frederick is very much taking Goa's rich history of print cultures first brought to Goa by the Jesuits in the sixteenth century and heritagizing it into the concept of the press itself. It is the small design details – such as the thoughtful naming of Goa,1556, including its lettering, font, and mirroring effect – that directly reference this point. Furthermore, the impressive series of books are design objects in and of themselves that take on an expanding range of heritage thematics (art, cuisine, culture, diaspora, Goana, music, novel, poetry, theatre, travelogue, to name some of them: see the very long list, www.goa1556.in/) as their central foci. In other words, it is Frederick's press that has directly contributed to an expansive secondary literature on a range of heritage topics (both tangible and intangible) that has greatly contributed to the reading for and writing of this ethnography on heritage and design in Goa. We could also consider Frederick's Goa,1556 a heritage press designed in such a way that it is always community-based; it is a range of Goan experts (both local and diasporic) who decide which heritage topics matter and are worthy of being written about and published.

Illustration by Orijit Sen, Goa. Copyright 2022.

6 Architecture

My sixth section is a portrait of Gerard da Cunha, who has worked on various design projects involving Goan architecture as heritage over the past twenty-five years. These include a book and small museum on the historic Indo-Portuguese-styled houses of Goa (1999), the recent controversial restoration of the sixteenth-century Portuguese Reis Magos Fort (2008), and lastly, the preservation of an archive and studio space dedicated to famed cartoonist Mario Miranda's (1926–2011) illustrations of daily Goan life. I have slowly come to know Gerard over a space of twenty years and have been observing (and now writing about) his evolving design ideas and architectural plans that very much show an enduring commitment to and investment in Goa as a place.

6.1 Houses of Goa

I first met Gerard da Cunha in May 1999 when I was living in Goa conducting fieldwork and archival research for my PhD dissertation on the expositions of St Francis Xavier. At the time, he was nearing completion on a book project, tentatively entitled *Houses of Goa*. It was a huge undertaking, several years in the making (1995–9), and one that involved members of staff from his architectural firm, a graphic designer (Rukshana Sarosh, who then became a close friend and features throughout this book), photographer Ashok Koshy, illustrator Sunita Dalvi, and two writers, Heta Pandit[8] and Annabelle Mascarenhas. It also included extensive field visits all over North and South Goa by this team of researchers to document a targeted set of Indo-Portuguese-styled Goan homes through sketches, drawings, and photographs. I attended the book launch for *Houses of Goa* (1999) in March 2000. It was a much-celebrated event with everyone who had worked so hard on its design in attendance. The result was a glossy, well-researched, beautifully illustrated coffee-table book that pays homage to Goa's rich architectural heritage in houses. In the foreword to the book, Gerard writes:

> What is it that makes Goan houses, both Hindu and Catholic, so special? For a start, it is their perfect placement in the landscape. Set history aside and it would seem that each village employed a sensitive urban designer (as the term rural designer does not exist in the architectural dictionary) who carefully placed the village green, the market and chose a strategic location for the village church ... the variety in the detail of the elements in these Goan

---

[8] Even as she is not profiled here, Heta Pandit is very much deserving of her own heritage portrait as an early pioneer and contributor, expanding Goa's heritage scene very early on by promoting heritage walks in and around Old Goa and its Indo-Portuguese houses and villages and writing a range of fascinating small heritage themed booklets (Da Cunha, Pandit, and Mascarenhas 1999; Pandit and Vakil 2003; Pandit 2004; Pandit and Rao 2006; Pandit 2008; Pandit 2015).

houses is astonishing. What made Goans channel all their energy in house building and construct every window, column, railing, gatepost, eavesboard and pilaster differently? . . . The ingredients were perfect for this amazing pot pourri – borrowings from the West and roots from the East in the hands of a people in search of their own identity. The end product? A domestic architecture comparable to the very best on Earth. (1999: 8)

Houses of Goa is an attempt to preserve the Goan house design, to methodically document it (and its design history) in a material sense in the face of impending change (political, economic, climatic) and an uncertain heritage landscape that could possibly include their future destruction or transformation into something else, a detail that Gerard da Cunha gestures to in his foreword above. Over a four-year period, Gerard and his architectural team researched over 150 Goan houses located in all corners of the state in meticulous detail to provide a general overview and historical sketch, with chapter titles such as 'From Mud to Marvels', 'A Way of Life', 'Elements of Style', 'House Forms', and 'Building the Goan House'. Throughout their study, the writers emphasize the central role of the Goan house in village life, for family reproduction and sociality, and with a wide range of design influences that reflect very much the Goan travelling way of life. They write:

> The Goan house, ranging from the simple basic shelter to the grand ornate mansion became a vital pivot on which family ties revolved. It gave its occupants and the members who were outside Goa a feeling of security, strength and permanence. As a result of this, many influences from Europe, Africa, and British-India crept into the building and embellishments of the houses of Goa . . . The money that flowed in from Portugal, Africa or British-India brought in by Goans scattered all over the world went into the most logical showcases – the houses . . . Along with the innovative ideas for mouldings, wall paintings, decorative windows, wall brackets and sconces came small artifacts – candlesticks, altar pieces, Western furniture, pottery, lamps, cut glass and bone china dinner-sets . . . Latin influences [were] introduced in the houses where the notion of space, areas of transition, and use of outdoor spaces still remained traditionally Indian. (1999: 32–3)

For the last chapter in the book, Gerard and his team selected a handful of houses (eight in total) from their larger survey, chosen for certain style elements. With a specific focus on 'the interplay of space and form' (1999: 94) for each of these houses and in relation to their present-day owners (including Mario de Miranda, who will come up again in this section), the book provides a balanced view of both the Goan Catholic and Hindu heritage house and offers up a remarkable series of 'Personality Profiles'. In their introduction to this last chapter, authors Pandit and Mascarenhas write: 'We've surveyed over a 150 houses and analysed them on the basis of their stylistic elements and their topological features. Some houses, however, defy scientific observation . . . we take a long and nostalgic look at these houses. We meet with house-owners and capture the emotional bonding they have with the houses they have occupied for generations. What we've come up with is much more than what we've deserved' (1999: 133). This last chapter is perhaps a fitting tribute to the remarkable heritage of Goa's houses that have endured; moreover, it serves as an important reminder that the Goan heritage house is also always a living, breathing, changing design space that adopts and adapts with the changing times.

Fast-forward thirteen years, and I am in Goa again for a five-month period to conduct research on my burgeoning project on heritage and design, only this time my family are in tow. We are looking for a school for our daughter to attend and are told by everyone in Goa to visit Nisha's Play School, which, it turns out, is run by Gerard's wife and is located directly across from Gerard's Gaudi-inspired home (his favourite architect he tells me on one occasion; it is a passion we both share for the Spanish architect) and next-door office space. Nisha gives us a tour of the ample and well-designed grounds, but in the end, there are no available openings for our daughter to attend her school. As we are leaving, I notice a new building on the premises and see a sign for Museum Houses of Goa, which is dedicated to the 'Houses of Goa' project that Gerard has designed and curated and based on the earlier research he had done for the book. I make a mental note and plan to go back another day on my own to visit the museum, which I do a week later. I pay the entrance fee of 100 rupees and enter a small two-storey sharply angled building that also cleverly functions as a traffic island, so as to not disrupt the daily flow of cars entering and exiting his wife's school for requisite child drop-offs and pick-ups. The museum is built in the shape of a triangle (and looks like a ship from the outside), with an expansive view onto the hilled plot of land that includes Nisha's school, the home that Gerard designed and lives in with his wife and two children, and his architectural office space which is located in a nearby separate building.

The museum, opened in 2004 (www.archgoa.org), tells the history of the Goan heritage house through material objects, drawings, text, and photographs. It is informative, detailed, and carefully designed (as was his earlier book) and includes two main gallery spaces, a reception area, café, bookshop, and a third gallery space that converts into a thirty-five-seat auditorium (Da Cunha 2004). It has been designed according to Gerard, as a 'resource cum research centre for the traditional architecture of Goa . . . We welcome any form of documentation, objects in the form of donation or on loan. The museum has no outside funding and is to be a self-sustaining project' (Da Cunha 2004). In addition, the museum has even bigger plans, for it 'intends conducting short-term workshops on the following subjects: 1. Traditional housing in Goa; 2. Creative design; 3. Innovative Construction' (Da Cunha 2004). On my way out, I pick up a cleverly designed fold-out brochure entitled 'Architect's note' that is on offer to members of the public, which details the construction ideas behind the building of the museum. In this architectural brief, Gerard opens up to his museum visitors, stating that his museum 'had to look "crazy" enough in the tradition of museum buildings (like the Guggenheim Bilbao or the Guggenheim New York) which would seduce the local vegetable seller into buying a ticket' (Da Cunha 2004). In this same brochure, Gerard reflects on various questions often asked by visitors, including why the metaphor of the ship. He confesses that it was 'quite accidental', but when he noticed it, he 'played along and added the waves' (Da Cunha 2004). Another concern often raised by visitors to his museum is that of 'why make such a modern building to house a subject which is so historical?' Gerard's response to this last question is fitting: 'I'll leave you to answer that one' (Da Cunha 2004), which in my mind is a fitting tribute to Gerard's design sensibility and Goa's dynamic heritage landscape, one that easily and innovatively blends the old and the new.

6.2 The Reis Magos Fort

It was during this same visit to Goa in 2013 that I sat down with Gerard at his office in the village of Salvador do Mundo to talk about his renovation of the heritage Reis Magos Fort, which he had been commissioned to take on in 2008, and which had caused much controversy over the almost four years it took to complete the design work.[9] The Reis Magos Fort (and church which was built at the base of the fort) is a much beloved sixteenth-century icon that dots the North Goan shoreline with its sweeping views of the Mandovi River from its position in the village of Reis Magos across the water from the capital city of Panjim. Historically, the Portuguese had commissioned the Franciscans to build the fort and church in 1551 on land that was once the site of an earlier Adil Shah of Bijapur fortification and armed outpost dating back to 1493 (www .reismagosfort.com). The Portuguese conquerors purposely placed the fort at the highest point on the hill due to its strategic position for controlling the mouth of the Mandovi River (where it meets the Indian Ocean), which then allowed them to anticipate any enemies (during this period it was the Dutch and Marathas) approaching by water. The fort was enlarged at different points (and re-erected in 1707) and endured during the longue durée of Portuguese

---

[9] My profile of heritage practitioner Gerard Da Cunha is based on various meetings with him in 2000 related to the Houses of Goa book project and interviews with him on 29 November 2013 and 27 May 2019.

colonialism (1510–1961), taking on a variety of functions – vice-regal residence, military fortress, site of Goa's British occupation (1798–1813), sometimes prison, infectious-disease hospital, and resting area. During the fight for independence from Portuguese colonial rule (1900–61), the Portuguese turned the fort into a jail to imprison Goa's freedom fighters. Post-1961, the Goan state government had retained its use as a prison, similar to nearby Fort Aguada (built in 1612) before finally abandoning it all together in 1993 (www .reismagosfort.com). It is these interstitial layers of the fort's architecture and functional history (including its abandonment) that showcase the legacy and monumentality of the Portuguese in Goa, and make it such a valued heritage site in Goa today, one that was very much in need of restoration by the time Gerard entered the scene and was asked to assess the fort's architectural condition in 2008.

Gerard tells me that it had been Mario de Miranda, whose ancestral house in the village of Loutilim he had profiled in his *Houses of Goa* book and who as the Goa representative for the Indian National Trust for Art and Cultural Heritage (INTACH; www.intach.org), a national governing body that oversees all tangible heritage renovation projects on the Indian subcontinent, had initially put forward Gerard's name for a list of potential architecture consultants to take on the much-needed restoration work at the fort. Gerard and Mario had become close friends in the process of designing the book project, and he pushed Gerard to submit a tender for the bid, believing him to be an ideal candidate to oversee and undertake this large-scale heritage project, given his specialization in Indo-Portuguese architecture. Despite several hurdles along the way, including the initial controversial procurement of outside funding from a wealthy British philanthropist Lord Hamish Hamlyn and his wife Helen, who had set up the Lady Helen Hamlyn Trust,[10] the restoration of the Reis Magos Fort into a heritage site and cultural centre was finally approved (including all the red tape involved in such a bureaucratic process) by the necessary INTACH officials. It was set to start construction work in late 2008 under the direction of Gerard da Cunha and his team of architects.

Because the fort had been used as a jail at various historical points in time to house different types of prisoners, Gerard first set about removing many of these layered add-ons in order to start his preservation work based on the original structure and layout of the fort. Once that was done, he tells me, he could then

---

[10] Very early on it was rumoured that Helen Hamlyn's motivation for providing the funds for its substantial renovation were in order to lease an apartment at the top level of the fort to be a private holiday home. Once this was confirmed to not be the case, the trust's donation was accepted for the work to begin. www.telegraph.co.uk/news/worldnews/asia/india/1413458/Tycoons-widow-loses-battle-to-restore-Goas-ancient-fort.html

focus his design ideas on the fort's 'restoration not alteration' (his words), which included installing glass panels to fortify crumbling walls, which would still allow for sweeping panoramic views of Panjim and the Mandovi River, placing concrete over rotting wooden floors, the cleaning and fixing of the corrugated tin roof, the smoothing out of all the stone floors and antique tilework, and lastly, the retention of mud walls. He also wanted to make the fort disability-accessible, which he considered an important design feature of the fort's restoration. In the end it took forty to fifty workers in his employment to complete the restoration work over a three- to four-year period and caused much controversy along the way, Gerard himself and the project inadvertently becoming the new target in a long-running heated debate over Goan and Indian heritage politics, including Goa's enduring Portuguese legacy and historic (Hindu) enemies, as well as larger factionalisms very present across the Indian subcontinent.

At one point, the Shiv Sena, a right-wing pro-Hindu political party opposed the renovation on the grounds both that the funds were coming from a British trust and that Gerard's design plans involved 1. installing a new lift structure and 2. adding modern amenities on the grounds of the historical fort (https://time sofindia.indiatimes.com/city/goa/Reis-Magos-fort-Plea-on-JMFC-order-rejected/articleshow/3943128.cms; https://mumbaimirror.indiatimes.com /news/india/not-with-british-cash-sena/articleshow/15833299.cms; https://eco nomictimes.indiatimes.com/news/politics-and-nation/shiv-sena-objects-govts-move-to-beautify-reis-magos-fort/articleshow/3256084.cms). According to the Shiv Sena, these two points violated Indian heritage rules, even suggesting that if Goa's central government could not pay for the renovation, they would instead. As a result, Gerard's restoration work was blocked from moving forward by the Goa police, many of his workers were threatened or attacked, and he was charged with defacement and damage to public property under the Ancient Monuments and Archaeological Sites and Remains Act (1978) by the Goan government (www.navhindtimes.com/story.php?story=2009020114).

In addition, Gerard tells me that the Goa Environmental and Ecology Trust (GEET) joined in on the protests; not only did they support the Shiv Sena's views that Gerard was violating heritage rules with the installation of a new structure on ancient grounds, but the old rumour resurfaced that he was in fact turning the fort into a holiday home for the British philanthropists Hamish and Helen Hamlyn. Eventually, these unfounded charges were dismissed in Goa's High Court, and Gerard was able to complete the restoration work, but he continued to do so behind locked doors and largely in the dead of night in order to prevent further vandalism to the valued heritage site. The fully restored Reis Magos Fort was opened to the public on 5 June 2012, with an attendance of over 250 people, including Gerard and his architectural team, and three former Goan freedom fighters who had been previously jailed in the fort (https://time-sofindia.indiatimes.com/city/goa/Restored-at-3-5-crore-Reis-Magos-fort-opens/articleshow/13858603.cms). Goa's Chief Minister Manohar Parrikar presided over the inaugural event, stating that 'we as a society should remember the past, adding that if we don't, that society can't build [a] defence for the future' (http://timesofindia.indiatimes.com/city/goa/Restored-at-3-5-crore-Reis-Magos-fort-opens/articleshow/13858603.cms).

Reflecting on the Reis Magos Fort project a year-and-a-half after its completion, in November 2013, Gerard tells me that he likes to think of monuments as sites of regeneration and empowerment for and in dialogue with a community, and that a successful renovation is one that honours heritage at the same time that it uses new technologies to modernize and make a heritage site accessible, practical, and sustainable for use in the now. Furthermore, it is these guiding principles of restoration work more generally that, in the end, proved a success as a model for opening the doors to additional renovation projects on heritage sites in and around Goa for Gerard. He has since been invited to give numerous lectures (and tours) on the basis of what is now regarded as his thoughtful design work on the fort, his marrying of commerce and heritage to create a sustainable economic model for other buildings in need of renovation work. His comments very much resonate for me as an ethics of care in design work that could very easily apply to the other heritage practitioners that I have chosen to profile in this book.

Three years later, I had the opportunity to spend an afternoon and evening at the restored Reis Magos Fort. I was visiting Goa in February 2015 to participate in GoaPhoto, a first-ever photo festival organized by Spanish-born Goan resident Lola Mac Dougall, who features in Section 7. Lola and her design team had transformed the grounds of the fort into an exhibition-cum-gallery space, with several photographic series beautifully curated into the renovated design of the fort. Gerard's vision for the Reis Magos Fort to become a Goan community-based cultural centre had come true in some sense.

6.3 Mario Miranda Gallery

Fast-forward six years (to 27 May 2019), and I have an appointment with Gerard to interview him at his office in the village of Salvador do Mundo (Torda), but this time in more depth about his range of design projects, past, present, and future. It is a long overdue visit, for after my meeting with him in 2013, in which the focus of our conversation had been largely his involvement in redesigning the Reis Magos Fort, I had tried again unsuccessfully to meet with him during a short visit to Goa in 2017, but he had been busy, flying overseas to do some commissioned design work. This time around, I have a better sense of what I want to talk about with him, which is first to profile his Mario Miranda Gallery space and archive project, and then to gain a better sense of his overall body of architectural work, including his future design plans.

While Gerard looks the same this time around, perhaps only slightly older, his architecture office looks very different, with Goan cartoonist Mario de Miranda prints, images, and merchandise taking over the space, almost overwhelming it. The 'Mario Gallery', as the front room is now named, started as a favour to Mario, he tells me. As I am a huge fan of Mario's famed cartoons (having met him on occasion during my fieldwork stint 1999 to 2000) and proud owner of his book *Goa With Love* (2001) – his cartoons say something about Goa with subtle humour and wit and complexity of caricature – I wanted to hear more about how Gerard entered the design world of cartoons from architecture. The point of connection is perhaps not so far off, according to Joanna Passos, Portuguese literary critic, Mario fan, colleague, and friend. She writes that 'beyond Mario's cosmopolitanism and his insightful perception of reality, another important aspect to consider in a general appreciation of his work is his undeniable passion for cultivating a dialogue with other arts, especially with architecture . . . When Mario de Miranda interprets a landscape, the composition reveals the eye of an architect instead of the vision of a painter' (2012: 243).

After the success of the *Houses of Goa* book, Mario had approached Gerard in the early 2000s (2003–4), asking him if he could design a book on his life in illustrations (1926–2011), one that would include a compilation of his social cartoons as commentary that spanned a forty-year illustrious career working for the *Times of India* newspaper group. Gerard agreed and started collecting everything he could find on Mario, meeting with and talking to people who knew him well, and building an archive of sorts that he enumerates at 8,000 drawings even as others have suggested a figure closer to 13,000 works of art – amounting, according to some estimates, to only 30 per cent of Mario's work (www.bbc.com/news/world-asia-india-36220327). This collection includes photographs of a number of murals he was commissioned to make over the years, which are well placed throughout Goa; a set of remarkable cartoon illustrations of daily life in Bombay (where Mario studied and worked) and Goa (the site of his ancestral home in Loutolim), including its heritage churches, houses, and villages, which featured in newspapers; various postcard series; illustrated diaries started from the age of fifteen (for the years 1949, 1950, 1951), and lastly, doodles from his travels abroad, created on overseas visits to Paris, London, New York, Macau, Japan, Portugal, and Germany.

Gerard then helped to organize a three-month-long exhibit of Mario's illustrated works in Panjim, and he timed it with the presale of his forthcoming
edited book, which was due to come out in July 2008. The book was a huge
success, he says, as he sold out of copies. Joanna Passos was visiting Goa at the
time of the exhibit and came across Mario's cartoon work for the first time at this
exhibit. She writes: 'Standing there, in front of his drawings, I was immediately
seduced by the amazing personality behind the art works, so deeply perceptive
of life and human nature' (Passos 2012: 242). But then Mario was diagnosed
with Parkinson's disease, lost his job working as an illustrator for the *Times of
India*, and needed an income. Gerard got involved to help out his close friend
and decided to start merchandising Mario's cartoons in order to generate
a regular income for him and his family. He produced a first series of five
books, compiling them into themes: *Mario's Goa* (2010e), *Mario's Travels*
(2010f), *Mario's Best Cartoons Book I* (2010b), *Mario's Bombay* (2010d),
Inside Goa (2010a), and *Mario's Best Cartoons Book II* (2010c). In the midst
of all this, Mario passed away from Parkinson's disease in December 2011.
Gerard persevered and designed a second series of three books based on his
diary illustrations from 1949, 1950, and 1951 (2016a, 2016b, 2016c).

In the aftermath of his death, Gerard also started up the Mario Gallery, taking
over the front room of his architectural office and filling it with original prints on
display in an upstairs area and with a limited range of Mario merchandise for
sale on the first floor, including prints, postcards, and pillows illustrated with
Mario's popular cartoon images. The Mario Gallery, both a physical space and
an online one (www.mariodemiranda.com), is also very much a design place
that pays homage to Goa's most beloved cartoonist, who is simultaneously
considered a Goan personality and a figure who heritagized Goa itself through
his design of cartoons as sharp social commentary.

More recently, in 2015, Gerard expanded the Mario brand into a business, setting
up a number of small shops (five in total) in different villages all over Goa
(Carmona, Calangute, Panjim, Margao, and Dabolim Airport), selling a range of
Mario books and expanded merchandise (including keyrings, t-shirts and dresses,
crockery, postcard reprints, and collectibles), with a percentage of the profits
continuing to go to Mario's widow Habiba and two sons. In a 2016 interview (on
what would have been on Mario's ninetieth birthday) with journalist Pamela
D'Mello (who is also the wife of publisher Frederick Noronha, who is featured
in Section 5), Gerard describes the famed Goan cartoonist as a 'versatile artist',
with a 'range of styles' and 'command over different mediums (colour, pen-and-
ink and charcoal) [making] him a bit of an enigma'. And though Mario 'gained
huge popularity during his lifetime, his true genius is yet to be recognized' (www
.bbc.com/news/world-asia-india-36220327). I myself own a Mario Miranda

screen-printed pillow that has pride of place on my office couch, its detailing of a Parisian café scene unfolding with wit, sly humour, and charisma, much like Mario himself.

Gerard's various heritagization projects showcased here should be seen as design work. Even as they involve renovation work, they are also always centred on design and a blending of the historic and contemporary in thoughtful ways, be it producing a book and building a small museum dedicated to Goa's heritage houses, transforming an old Portuguese fort into a new public centre, or creating a visual archive of Mario Miranda's drawings, sketches, and cartoons of Goan daily life, one that sustains itself commercially. Gerard continues to follow this same ethos in a range of new architecture and design projects, both large and small, including the renovation of the Old Portuguese Secretariat (formerly the Adil Shah Palace) located in downtown Panjim, which has now been transformed into a successful events space that hosts the annual Serendipity Festival of the Arts (www.incrediblegoa.org/focus/goas-adil-shah-palace-gets-complete-facelift-serendipityartsfestival/) and which featured Orijit Sen's Mapping Mapusa Market project, the subject of Section 3. He is also renovating a historic fort in Setubal, Portugal (modelled on the success of his Reis Magos Fort work) and designing a housing project in nearby Hampi for a steel-manufacturing company, Jindal South West (JSW), which involves building 2,000 small housing units for its employees. Smaller projects include designing two private residences – one is a small house for some clients in Vasco (Goa), and another is a large mansion that incorporates natural forms for a billionaire client in Alibagh, India.

Lastly, Gerard has also slowly been working on his grand plan to build a museum dedicated to Indian architecture, something that does not yet exist on the subcontinent, a fact he tells me is quite incredible. He still needs to raise the funds to build it, but in the meantime, he has reserved a 1.5 acre, 6,000 m^2 plot of land he owns near his office for its future location. Knowing Gerard, and despite the fact that it is perhaps his biggest design project to date, he will make it happen, and I will most likely get a personal tour on my next visit to Goa. I come away from our meeting feeling hopeful that I have energized Gerard with all my questions. Perhaps I pushed him out of his specialized world of architecture, even if only temporarily, to realize how much he has done (and evolved in a design sense) to design and contribute to Goa's architectural heritage landscape.

Illustration by Orijit Sen, Goa. Copyright 2022.

7 Village

7.1 Introduction

My seventh section is a portrait of Goa's villages as a heritage and design space, places where I have lived and worked alongside many creative persons. I know some of these villages intimately, having spent time experiencing daily life in Saligao (2013, 2017), Chikhli (2018), and Moira (2019). I begin this section with what I call a village interlude, which I offer as a slight detour, a side journey into some personal reflections on Goa's hinterland and ways of being. The section is also a portrait of two individuals who live in and take up the Goan villages as sites and sets for their respective design projects. Lola Mac Dougall is an Argentinian-Spanish curator and photography specialist whom I met in 2013 while living in Goa over a five-month period. Lola has lived in several villages – Bastora, Aldona, and Moira – over the nine years that I have known her, after moving from Delhi with her husband and young son. Over this period, she has fashioned Goa's architectural landscape (including its Indo-Portuguese Catholic churches, houses, and village interiors) as backdrops for her biannual international photography festivals. While I was involved in the organization of both the first and second GoaPhotos (2015 and 2017), my focus will be on the latter one that took place in November 2017 and which showcased the village of Saligao, its heritage very much on display alongside photography. This section is equally a portrait of writer and artist Savia Viegas, whom I met and inter-viewed in Carmona in May 2019. Savia uses her ancestral village (to which she returned after living many years in Mumbai) as the setting for her fiction, paintings, and the starting-up of a local primary school. By way of organization, I first elaborate on the concept of the village as a marker of Goa's Indo-Portuguese heritage, before turning to these two design projects[11] set in two distinct villages, one located in North Goa and the other in South Goa, historic-ally distinct regions with differing relationships to tourism and heritage.[12]

---

[11] My profile of heritage practitioner Lola Mac Dougall is based on fieldwork in Goa over five months in 2013, two weeks in 2015 (25 February 25–7 March), eleven days in 2017 (17–27 November), and two months in 2019 (April–May). My profile of heritage practitioner Savia Viegas is based on fieldwork in Goa during two months in 2019 (April–May), including a formal interview at her house on 30 May 2019.

[12] There is a much longer history to North versus South Goa tied to the colonial and missionary history of Old and New Conquests in Goa and the regional influences of conversion and religious practices (Hinduism, Catholicism, and Islam) in the shaping of cities and village life. Postcolonial infrastructures of tourism and heritage preservation were concentrated initially more in and around North Goa due to the location of the seat of the Portuguese colonial capital first in Old Goa and then its transfer to the newly built city of Nova Goa (Panjim) beginning in the mid-eighteenth century, with its status as the new capital of Portuguese India taking place in 1843. However, it is now changing, with the South increasingly rivalling the North as a site for high-end tourism development and heritage building (Trichur 2013).

In this section, I approach Goa's villages as both a marker of its heritage and as a site for several design projects.

7.2 Village Interlude

For two weeks in February 2018, I organized a writer's residency for myself, staying in the very small remote northern village of Chikhli. My initial thought had been that, if I was going to write about living in Goa's hinterland, I had better try it myself. I arrive in the middle of the night from my flight on Qatar Airlines, unsure as to the taxi's destination, a place called Casa Colvale, a resort hotel near to where I am staying the only marker found on Google Maps. I am eventually led into a small, quaint studio space, painted a deep blue on the outside and appropriately named Little Xanti ('peace' in Konkani). It is a sort of cottage built into the front garden of a larger house that looms overhead with its two storeys and expansive view onto the nearby paddy fields. The house belongs to Gopika and Raag, a graphic artist and architect couple who live and work between Delhi and Goa and organize artist residencies throughout the year, www.facebook.com/littlexanti/), excepting the months of December and January, when they reserve the cottage space for their extended family holidays. Even though I never meet them during my stay, I gain a sense of their creative lives (in the furniture, the views, the simplicity of their style, the use of natural elements for decoration) each time I go over to their house to borrow some milk or sugar. They have employed Reena and Amos, a newly married local couple, as caretakers in their stead. I am also introduced to Hubert and Annie, who live several houses down on the narrow alleyway and charge 125 rupees for a fresh tiffin of Goan curry and rice, a heritage staple (Gracias 2012) that I would eat on more than one occasion.

I would write in the mornings, do yoga on the outside porch in the afternoons, and go for walks at sunset, seeing how the light would change the view onto the rice fields. I hardly see any other people during this period of quietude, but I see plenty of peacocks, cows, and birds. I am also told there are crocodiles across the way. I venture out of the village on occasion, one day walking towards but not quite reaching the nearby village of Colvale where Wendell Rodricks, who features in Section 4, has his home. Another day, I turn in the opposite direction on my walk and cross a *bund* (embankment) through a field of mangroves on a patch of narrow ground, before I approach the village of Curilim, where a huge silver-coloured snake crosses my path inside the old church grounds. On my return, I pass a liquor shop selling a local Goan *toddi* that I buy as a present to take back home for my rum-drinking partner. On another day, I find the local bus stop with its requisite general store run by wife Pooja and husband Prasant.

I would pick up my eggs and daily fresh *pao* there and recharge my cell phone as I waited for the bus to show up. According to Pooja, the local bus is infrequent and does not follow a scheduled run at the best of times. I would sit on a bench in the shade of the general store, whilst I wait for the bus (or rather any bus) to appear around the bend – its list of various corner stops hand-painted in cursive on the side of the bus in Konkani only, which I have never seen before, as English is typically the language of written communication throughout Goa. This small detail serves as a reminder of how localized and deep in the interior of Goa's hinterland this majority Konkani-speaking village is located.

7.3 GoaPhoto

Saligao is a Goan village I have come to know well and appreciate, having lived in close proximity for five months in a rented flat with my family from August 2013 to January 2014. I would enjoy the daily morning drive as I would leave the coastal belt and meander through nestled trees and winding roads to drop off my then-two-year-old daughter at her school, called Tiny Tots. It was run by a gentle woman named Lorraine, who housed the school in the front room of her home down a side alleyway in Saligao. It was daily acts involving timed outings and driving routines, such as the organization of childcare, that also inevitably became part of the ethnographic research for this book. It is the same village I returned to and stayed in for two weeks in 2017 to help out with organizing GoaPhoto from 23 to 25 November, an international photography festival that was conceptualized by Lola Mac Dougall (www.goaphoto.in). I had first met Lola in 2013, having been introduced to her through mutual friends at a dinner party. She and her husband (Goan ancestry, Indian-born, Paris-raised) had met in Delhi when she was based there working for the Spanish Consulate. After living in India's capital for five years, they had decided to move to Goa with their young son, in search of a less hectic lifestyle. They first settled in the village of Bastora and rented a Goan house while they looked for a property to buy and build their dream house. Lola also started doing a PhD at a Spanish university, which would eventually involve me as an external advisor; her topic was three female Indian photographers: Gauri Gill, Ketaki Sheth, and Dayanita Singh, a photographer who was also based in Goa. As Lola settled into a Goan lifestyle and started planning the research for her PhD, she saw a niche for an arts festival dedicated to photography, which was also conceived of as a heritage event. It was a slow process to build networks in a new place and secure international funding to bring a range of international photographers, but she and her husband Nikhil were successful in their endeavours and organized the first GoaPhoto that took place over two weeks from 25 February to 7 March 2015 and which I was involved in as the convenor of a panel on gender and photography and an essay contributor to the catalogue (on Mexico-based Alinka Echeverria's series entitled 'The Road to Tepeyac') produced alongside the exhibit (www.goaphoto.in/2015/; Gupta 2015).

Spanish-born curator Frank Kalero, based in Brazil and also a close friend of Lola's, was put in charge. Appropriately named 'The Other', the festival showcased nineteen 'other' photographers (from Belgium, Spain, India, the USA, Mexico, Chile, South Africa, Germany, Portugal, Switzerland, Finland, Japan, and Argentina) inside Goa's capital city of Panjim, using many of its urban heritage buildings as sets for a range of photography series of different shapes and sizes. There were large-format photographs staged in unlikely places – the unwieldy staircase of the Portuguese Baroque Immaculate Conception Church, the outside garden of Kala Academy, which is a public hall-cum-performance area, and on the sixteenth-century bricked grounds of the recently renovated (by Gerard da Cunha, who is featured in Section 6) Portuguese Reis Magos Fort, overlooking the Indian Ocean as the incoming wind flapped the images around. As Lola writes in the introduction to the GoaPhoto catalogue produced alongside the festival:

> GOAPHOTO is a finely curated international photography festival to be held each year ... Citizens and visitors will have the opportunity to interact with photography in an unconventional manner, as most of the exhibitions will be presented in public spaces and in large formats. The nineteen exhibitions ... are an invitation to promenade ... and to be surprised by both fine art photography and the uniqueness of Panaji's heritage and character.
>
> (Mac Dougall 2015: 10)

Much the same as Lola employed the city of Panjim and its heritage as the set design for her first GoaPhoto festival in 2015, she carried on with this theme the next time around, deciding to fashion the village of Saligao and its heritage buildings (including its houses and churches) in North Goa as the set design for her second GoaPhoto festival, which took place from 23 to 26 November 2017 (www.goaphoto.in/2017/). I also attended and was involved in setting up this second event, purposely staying in Saligao during the days preceding it and up until its closing ceremony so as to gain a better sense of the how the village itself was getting 'dressed up' for these festival days. With less funding this time around to bring a range of international photographers, this GoaPhoto was staged on a smaller scale and felt more intimate, with the chosen theme of

'Domesticities'. In her introduction to the GoaPhoto Catalogue for this second festival, entitled 'House Taken Over', Lola writes:

> GoaPhoto is an international photography festival that produces location-specific installations connecting photographic displays and their architectural contexts. Goa, the smallest Indian state, is an idiosyncratic region within the Subcontinent. There are abundant material traces of the Portuguese rule in the region, which spanned across five centuries and officially ended in 1961. However, there are lesser-known treasures to be found in its private architecture, which is for the most part inaccessible: within Goan homes one may encounter one of the most valuable aspects of this region's patrimony ... because many of these homes continue to be lived in and used as residences, the project proposed an innovative approach to working with 'living heritage'. (Mac Dougall 2017: no pages)

I wandered the narrow streets of Saligao, redolent in its heritage, and visited house upon house (including the Red and Ochre Corner House, Quinta Serena, the House of White Crabs, and the House of Enquiry) following the detailed hand-drawn village map that had been included in the festival programme and handed out to participants so that no one would miss out or get lost along the way. It marked the various photo exhibits quietly on display inside a range of interior spaces, including living rooms, bedsits, gardens, and terraces. I saw an ageing typewriter being used to prop up a photograph in one home; in another, a foyer bench held a set of four themed photographs. An old wicker chair in a different house had a cushion with a photo printed on it, and an antique four-poster bed had a set of dramatic drapes consisting of blown-up facial images on its two sides. I came to realize that Lola had pushed further the idea of using heritage as the set and setting for design during this second GoaPhoto, including its exclusive focus on and access to interiority. She writes:

> We requested six curators to explore the theme of 'the domestic' and to respond to the location their exhibitions would inhabit, as the private spaces that constituted our venues retained their in situ furniture: it was a case of two aesthetics – the photographic and the domestic engaging with each other. What kind of exhibition can occupy a snake box in the house of a set designer? Can the two-seater palanquin that receives visitors in one of the residencies be used as a frame for a Mexican photo essay? Can we highlight the cosiness (sic) of a visiting room by displaying an exhibition on cushions? Is exhibiting in a kitchen going too far? Are we serious? These were some of the questions that came to mind while testing site-specificity inside domestic spaces, assigning a central stage to the objects that inhabited them, and in the process, attributing to them almost animistic qualities.
>
> (Mac Dougall 2017: no pages).

With the domestic and the photographic engaged in a visual dialogue inside various lived ancestral homes located in the village of Saligao, GoaPhoto 2017 showcased perfectly the potential of heritage to be used as the setting for a range of contemporary visual design projects, as well as the ability to work creatively with and inside living heritage in order to perform itself, showcasing both ancestral homes and contemporary photography equally to a larger Goan community. Furthermore, Lola's hand-drawn maps for her participant-observation walking tours in the village of Saligao worked much like the way Orijit's did for his Mapping Mapusa project (featured in Section 3), both as a form of experiential memory-making and storytelling (of a village, its changing lifeworld, and cast of characters). Her GoaPhoto series also potentially opens up new heritage processes by way of a combination of methodologies and design ideas: walking, mapping, ethnography, and photography. Lola Mac Dougall would continue to employ this same conceptual framing, using the village of Aldona (where she had lived for several years and had come to know intimately, both its interior and exterior spaces) as the set design and performance stage for her third biannual GoaPhoto that was staged over three days (6–8 December 2019; www.goaphoto.in/2019/). I was sorry to miss the festival this time around.

7.4 Fiction, Painting, and the Colour Blue

I first meet Savia Viegas at her village house in Carmona, South Goa in May 2019. I had been told earlier by Diviya Kapur, owner of Literati whom I profile in Section 5, that I must meet Savia and interview her about her life in writing and painting for my heritage project. In the interim, I purchase a copy of Savia's latest book, *Song Sung Blue* (2018), and read it over a few days. It holds my attention and makes a visceral impression on me. I immediately understand why Diviya has suggested that we two meet, as well as the fact that I am too focused on the north while there is a whole world of heritage and design happening in South Goa's hinterland.[13] I hire a car with a driver for the day and go for a languid two-hour drive, bypassing Panjim, crossing over the Zuari bridge, which serves as a divide between North and South Goa, circling Margao (Goa's second-largest city after Panjim), and seeing signs for villages with names like Verna, Majorda, and Varca.

---

[13] Even as my point in this section is to insert South Goa into the larger conversation on heritage and design in Goa by way of my portrait of Savia Viegas, the south features less prominently in my book due to my own long-term familiarity with the north over a twenty-five-year period. An example of another South Goa-based heritage maker worthy of a profile but not included here would be Victor Hugo Gomes, who runs the Goa Chitra Museum, a fascinating Goan heritage project (including an ethnographic collection) located in South Goa in the village of Benaulim (www.goachitra.com/). I went on a guided tour of the museum during my fieldwork in May 2019.

The driver gets lost a few times before we land up in the village of Carmona, and at Savia's doorstep, by late morning. We had earlier stopped by the famous Jila Bakery (https://lbb.in/goa/plum-cake-eclairs-jila-bakery/) in the village of Camorlim to buy some fresh Goan eclairs to bring as a gift. As we sit together in her light-filled workspace located in the back of what was once her father's ancestral home, we talk non-stop over a three-hour period.

Savia tells me her life story over coffee and éclairs, one that started in the village of Carmona as a sickly child born in 1957 (and with a sister who later joined a nunnery), four years before Goan independence from Portuguese colonial rule in the very house where we are seated. She eventually outgrew her sickly state, despite 'all the quack doctors' that treated her until the age of twelve, and then left the narrow confines of what she considered Goan village life – or what she described to me as her 'state of somnambulism growing up in Goa', moving to Mumbai to study English literature and Indology. Her new city and home made her 'aware and awake', she tells me. She wanted to move beyond her sleepy Goan-ness, which started with small things like replacing her Goan Western-styled dresses with the wearing of saris, in order to adopt a 'woke' pan-Indian metropolitan identity. She also met and fell in love with a journalist along the way and became one herself, working for the *Times of India* for several years (from 1981 to 1984) before deciding to take up teaching and a PhD in Indology studies whilst raising two young sons. She completed her PhD in 2000 and started up a Heritage Studies program, the first of its kind in Mumbai, but eventually left it after several years as it became mired in criticism due to internal politics.

Savia turned instead to a career in research and writing, developing first a project on the Prince of Wales Museum in Mumbai that profiled its international visitors (funded by the Fulbright Foundation) and another on collecting Goan family photographs (funded by a Government of India grant). It was this second research project that made her return to her roots in 2005, staying in Carmona and driving around Goa in a beat-up old car, taking photos of Goan family albums with her newly purchased Canon camera. She never asked for the original prints or the negatives, as she thought that they should rightfully stay with their owners. She tells me how she has approximately 700 photographs in her collection and is still trying to finish writing a book on these found images, a small sampling of which I had seen on display at Subodh Kerkar's Museum of Goa (MOG, in Pilerne (www.museumofgoa.com/)) earlier in the month of May. Savia is also near to completion on developing a scholarly book on the early twentieth-century Goan painter Angelo de Fonseca, who is best known for nativizing the Christian figure of Mary by painting her wearing an iconic Indian sari. As I listen to her life story, I see someone seated across the sofa in front of me who is thriving in a village setting, juggling several different art projects that are enriching and give so much back to Goa. I am reminded of the busy-ness that animated Gerard da Cunha, the architect who is profiled in Section 6.

Our conversation turns to her fiction, and how she landed up back in Goa, becoming a writer and painter. She tells me that it was her Goa photography project that slowly pulled her back to Carmona. As she travelled around documenting family photographs, she discovered a new-found earnestness in Goa, an investment in art and literature, a creative energy and impulse that compelled her to give the place and space another try. It was the year 2005, and she was spending most of her time back in Goa. By 2007, she and her family (a husband and two adult sons) had settled back fully in Goa, and in the village of Carmona where she had recently inherited her father's family home. She tells me how at that point, she 'put her paws into writing and painting' and that she was 'landscaping Goa' in her fiction books. She also set up the Saxtti (the name for the region of Salcette in Konkani) Foundation Trust as a response to Penguin Books changing its mind on publishing her first novel, *Tales from the Attic* (2007), set in her home village of Carmona, Salcette. Her next book, *Let Me Tell You About Quinta* (2011), was published by Penguin Books. She also started painting, and in 2009 she organized an exhibit entitled 'Picturing Us' (many of the paintings depicting village spaces and characters) inside her house; it was a success, with all twenty-eight paintings on display sold out (www.saviaviegas.in/painting.html).

We finally get to the subject at hand, which initially drew me to her work, her elegiac book *Song Sung Blue* (2018). For me, her novel perfectly shows how Carmona, standing in for Goan village life more generally, is a heritage object that is under threat of disappearance. Carmona is also the design set for a series of paintings that accompany the text but also stand alone as a visual story unto itself, for whose palette she chose the colour blue. It is both Savia's text and illustrations that we discuss in detail, her responses to me mirrored in many of her online interviews which also showcase her lively presence and articulate speech (both in person and online). In a recent review of her book (20 May 2019), fellow Goan writer Augusto Pinto writes:

> The illustrated novella *Song Sung Blue*, the fifth and latest offering of author, artist and academic Savia Viegas borrows its title from Neil Diamond's 1972 number 1 hit song of the same name. In it Diamond sings: 'Me and you are subject to the blues now and then / But when you take the blues and make a song / You sing them out again', suggesting that turning sadness into art can be cathartic ... This is what [her] writing and painting attempts to achieve. (www.joaoroqueliteraryjournal.com/review-events-new/2019/5/20/song-sung-blue-by-savia-viegas).

Just as Pinto reminds us of Savia's naming of her novel based on a song, musical theatre also frames the structure of the novel itself. In a 2019 review for *Scroll India*, Nandita Dutta describes Savia's experimental work as 'narrated like a tiatr (tiatr, derived from the Portuguese word "teatro" is a form of musical theatre popular in Goa), comprising 14 acts – only, the songs have been replaced in the book by artwork' (https://scroll.in/article/ 923000/this-dark-tale-from-goa-told-in-words-and-pictures-is-made-less-menacing-by-detached-storytelling). Savia also explains her choice of the village of Carmona as the setting for most of her novels, including *Song Sung Blue*. In a 2019 online interview for the *Joao-Roque Literary Journal* with Goan writer Selma Carvalho, she states:

> As a sickly child brought up in a sheltered environment, I would often lie in bed imagining life in an Arcadian paradise. This was a serious obsession in childhood. When I began writing fiction in my forties, the hunt began for a place where I could posit my characters. The location had to have the rich density like Gabriel Garcia Marquez' *Macondo* or R. K. Narayan's, *Malgudi*. Unlike the above-mentioned literary settings, however, Carmona was not a nondescript village, but a living, breathing entity, a village with 1,000 homes . . . The village was a microcosm for Goa'.
> (www.joaoroqueliteraryjournal.com/nonfiction-1/2019/2/18/mz9x48s8rbvqi 6ionmxbjliyo6l36a)

Not only does Carmona stand in for all Goan villages, but her readers also think so, many of them telling Savia the writer that 'the stories from [her] books are the stories from their village[s]' (www.joaoroqueliteraryjournal.com/nonfiction-1/ 2019/2/18/mz9x48s8rbvqi6ionmxbjliyo6l36a). Furthermore, her novels reflect the tensions between old and new taking place in Goa's villages today, and what Selma Carvalho describes as the 'death of culture in Goan villages which lie outside the periphery of the Panjim belt' (www.joaoroqueliteraryjournal.com/nonfiction-1/ 2019/2/18/mz9x48s8rbvqi6ionmxbjliyo6l36a). In response to Selma's point, Savia writes:

> The irony is that the genteel culture which was the hallmark of Goa's villages is now no more. The brash culture that has succeeded it has muscle and decibel power. Those that fear a confrontation move over to the main cities of Pangim [in the north] and Margao [in the south] where this brashness has less impact . . . The only vestige of the past that remains in the vast countryside is the architecture, a silent reminder of a homeland and the city, like Noah's Ark which saves all the precious species from the deluge.
> (www.joaoroqueliteraryjournal.com/nonfiction-1/2019/2/18/mz9x48s8rbvqi 6ionmxbjliyo6l36a).

With a careful crafting of words, the Goan village is shown to be an increasingly hollowed heritage object that Savia recuperates (and hallows) in some sense by both living inside and writing about it, setting her fiction inside its complex folds.

I now turn to her series of paintings that accompany the writing in *Song Sung Blue* and that make an immediate impression on me; I find them starkly beautiful, as they say so much more about the complex interior lives of her cast of Goan characters. I am surprised when Savia tells me that she is a self-taught painter. She likes to think visually she says, completing the writing first, and then the series of paintings that illustrate the text; it is a form of 'release to the images that build up as she works on her fiction', she states online (www.saviaviegas.in). Furthermore, her blue paintings have been exhibited in Portugal twice, in 2017 at the University of Lisbon and in 2018 in the village of Louem in the Algarve region. I am reminded of Gita Chadha's apt description of Savia's earlier 2009 paintings as a form of 'visual ethnography' (www.saviaviegas.in/gita_chadha.html); it is equally applicable to this series, for they articulate my own anthropological inter-pretation of her artwork, with their focus on what is felt rather than stated.

Savia also expands on her chosen palette. She writes:

> I chose blue thinking it would be cheaper to print. On experimenting, I loved [it] – the range is amazing. Indigo, Cerulean, Teal, Peacock, Prussian and Royal blue among others. Personal sufferings are refracted through the colour blue by many painters and filmmakers ... The best depths of blue are found in Moghul miniatures. Picasso drew heavily in postures and gestures from Christian iconography to depict daily life and reality. Yes, Picasso's oeuvre during this period did focus on social outsiders whether they were prisoners, beggars, circus people or the poor. Having been raised in a conservative Roman Catholic household, the visual canon of Christian iconography is deeply embedded in the core of my creative being ... In a way, *Song Sung Blue* uses the prism of religion and social convention to refract light on its social 'Others'. (www.joaoroqueliteraryjournal.com/nonfiction-1/2019/2/18/mz9x48s8rbvqi 6ionmxbjliyo6l36a).

For Savia, the colour blue refracts all the worldly influences of a range of historic artists (including musicians, painters, and filmmakers) on her own palette; it also says so much about dwelling inside Goa's villages, as felt, sensorial, sonic, and lived heritage, including its basis in Roman Catholic iconography and Portuguese *fado* (blues) music. In other words, 'blue' becomes the affective colour of Goa's heritage (Meloy 2002; Solnit 2005; Ali 2006; Cahen 2012; Gupta 2018a), its expressive melancholic and musical (and perhaps even religious for some) quality for a range of persons dwelling in its hinterland. More generally, it is the fading, emptying out of Goan village life (and as increasingly labelled 'other') that Savia importantly represents and resurrects through the twinned acts of writing and painting, for herself and her readers, and includes a number of Goans living in Goa and/or abroad. She inhabits and performs a Goan village way of life, suggesting an ethics of return by way of (her own) life example, one that also suggests its enduring value and viability for Goa's future generations.

Savia and I end our half-day together with a Goan style fish curry and rice lunch, accompanied by her charming husband, and a walking tour of her latest project, the moving of SaxttiKids (www.saviaviegas.in/saxtti.html), the primary school she had started up a few years earlier, to its new premises, the recently renovated village home of her grandmother in Carmona. It is the school her three granddaughters currently attend. My interview, alongside this series of online exchanges and responses, works in a multimodal manner, and helps fill in this portrait of a writer and painter very much at home in the world. It also suggests in many ways the larger point I am trying to convey in this section: the creative ways in which Lola Mac Dougall and Savia Viegas both utilize the idea and materiality of the Goan village and recognize its potential as a heritage object, very much employing living heritage whilst performing and designing it in some sense for more contemporary usages through the mediums of the visual and textual combined – involving photography, fiction writing, and painting. For Lola, the village homes of Saligao provide a series of creative heritage sets for a photo festival, and for Savia, the village of Carmona provides a plot, setting and canvas for the life of a Goan fictional character named Divina, whose life is a song sung blue.

AFTERWORD:
GOA BY DESIGN

Illustration by Orijit Sen, Goa. Copyright 2022.

8 Afterword: Goa by Design

This Element has been about exploring a dynamic heritage and design landscape in a globalized place called Goa. It offers up a series of portraits of an exciting range of contemporary heritage makers involved in five themed design projects (market, cloth, book, architecture, village) suggesting in some sense that they play a central role in transforming Goa's hinterland into an innovative design and studio space that is very much in process. These creative persons are equally committed to designing Goa's heritage futures, making for an enriched way of life that leads by example and that thinks carefully about old and new, and sustainable and ethical design aspects, choices, and materials in the Anthropocene, a geological era of dwindling natural resources, particularly 'monsoonal wetness' in the case of Goa (Gupta 2021). It includes, for example, the way Savio Jon relies on natural organic dyed cottons produced only in India for his clothing line, and the glass panels that Gerard da Cunha thoughtfully installed inside the interior walls of the Reis Magos Fort as a means to include more expansive views onto the Indian Ocean from atop. Furthermore, it involves the manner in which Goa's villages become the clever set designs for GoaPhoto under the discerning eye of curator Lola Mac Dougall, and the way that Orijit Sen creatively maps the Mapusa market as forms of memory-making and storytelling that counter globalized mall culture to focus on locally produced goods and repair work instead. Lastly, it is in the style by which Frederick has designed a small independent heritage book press to preserve Goa's heritage in print *by* and *for* a community base. These acts of portraiture also reveal as much about the changing heritage-scape of Goa as they do about the evolving creative practices of these heritage practitioners over a twenty-five-year period.

This Element shows how Savia Viegas started out as a journalist working in Mumbai and then studied Indology and started up a heritage programme, before returning to her Goan roots in her ancestral village of Carmona in South Goa to become a fiction writer and painter. It traces how architect Gerard da Cunha started out designing a book on the Indo-Portuguese heritage houses of Goa, before moving onto other projects during the span of his career, which includes the production of a visual and commercial archive to honour his close friend, famed Goan cartoonist Mario Miranda. It is about Wendell Rodrick's career as a clothing designer, one that involves sewing Goa into his resort wear, writing a memoir and producing a book on Goan sartorial history, and finally opening up a costume museum and research centre as his enduring legacy. These globalized locals have taken inspiration from Goa's heritage landscape (both tangible and intangible) and interpreted it into a range of contemporary design objects. Moreover, the majority of them have journeyed to or arrived in Goa by way of elsewhere, bringing their diverse educational training and experiences abroad with them. They came initially in search of an alternative cosmopolitanism to be found inside Goa and are, in some sense, actively producing and shaping the contours of that alternative cosmopolitanism itself.

Furthermore, this multifaceted group of persons and personalities make up a vibrant Goan collective of heritage makers who are shaped by and complement one another's design ideas. Not only are they sometimes involved in or connected to one another's heritage projects, but they often lend a helping hand on occasion and have developed enduring relationships along the way. They are in some sense each other's customers, clients, and discerning publics. The Element maps out how Gerard first met Mario Miranda, for it was his Goan heritage house that is featured in his *Houses of Goa* book and that solidified a life-long friendship. It is the way that Diviya gave Frederick a discount on his purchase of second-hand children's books once she heard of his new lending library plan for Saligao's youngest readers. It is no coincidence that Orijit's art displays of his Mapping Mapusa Market project are exhibited at the Serendipity Arts Festival, in the newly designed heritage art space that Gerard da Cunha was commissioned to undertake. It is the way that Savio trained with Wendell for a few years, developing a friendship and mutual respect for one another out of what was initially a mentor/student relationship. Equally, it is about the deep friendship that is visible when one sees Sacha and Savio in the same room, and the way they play with and tease out their creative ambitions and ideas with one another.

These heritage practitioners are also a friendly group of individuals, always welcoming to newcomers like myself to get involved in their exciting design projects, even at the smallest level. It is the way I become a teaching assistant for Orijit Sen's short course at Goa University or spend a rainy Sunday driving around South Goa in Diviya's *Bebook* van, handing out books as part of its outreach mobile lending library. It is the way I am inspired to contribute a piece for Lola's GoaPhoto Catalogue on the visual display of Elinka Echeverria's Mexico photographs inside a Goan Catholic church, or the way Diviya tells me that I must meet Savia Viegas, for her commitment to preserving the heritage landscape of South Goa and designing the village into her fiction writing and painting. In other words, it has also been remarkable for me to witness the determination, tenacity, and generosity with which these heritage makers pursue their Goa dreams, learning from one another's design experiments, the failures and successes both, and welcoming strangers (like myself) along the way.

These heritage designers are equally invested in giving back to a larger Goan public, both the one living in Goa and that of its globalized (and online) diaspora. It is the primary school that Savia opens up in the grounds of her grandmother's ancestral home in the village of Carmona, or the way that Gerard designs his Houses of Goa Museum in a manner that he hopes will 'seduce the local vegetable seller to come take a peek'. It is the way in which Orijit's visual maps tell Goan stories, equally of buyers and vendors of the Mapusa market, so that they see themselves reflected in his public artworks. It is also the lively digital personalities that Orijit and Wendell have both designed online, and which suggest a larger global following, one that taps into and includes an active Goan diaspora. It is the way that Frederick's heritage press is designed by and for members of Goa's reading public, with every Goan, according to him, 'having at least one book in them to write'.

There is also a Konkani language-based heritage world forming in Goa's hinterland that I have gestured to in small acts throughout this book, in the way that Diviya initially sourced Konkani books for Literati or that Frederick is very cognizant of this other lively press and growing scholarship, and by the fact that the hand-painted list of stops on the side of the bus in Chikhli where I stayed for two weeks were written in Konkani only. In other words, even as the set of persons presented here are designing Goa's heritage largely through the medium language of English (and Portuguese to some extent), there is another space of a Konkani-language heritage that I am aware of, and recognize its enduring value and changing landscape. It is Gerard who mentions to me during our last interview that he likes to think of heritage as sites of regeneration and empowerment for and in dialogue with a community, and that a successful design project is one that honours its past at the same time that it uses new technologies to modernize and make a particular heritage site accessible, practical, and sustainable for use in the here and now. His comments very much resonate for me as an ethics of care and giving back in design work that could very easily apply to the other heritage makers that I have chosen to showcase in this book.

This thriving community located in the hinterland is also very much guiding Goa's future iterations of heritage and design, which I suspect will continue to grow and develop in interesting and surprising ways. Even as I can only gesture to its future in broad strokes to be one of renewed investment and a sense of resilience in the face of the ongoing Covid pandemic, it will most likely be innovative, combining this set of heritage makers and shakers alongside a newer younger set of designers. They will take inspiration from the groundwork that has already been put in place by this former group of thoughtful and creative persons in order to ponder heritage and design in exciting and complex, personalized and political ways.

During my last visit to Goa in June 2019, I attend a dinner party at Lola's stylish home and meet a new cast of characters who want to make Goa their home in the near future, drawn to its inspirational design work centred on heritage, aspects of which have also made me commit to this special place over the longue durée, just as it has the many others, past, present, and future. Hence the set of heritage portraits I offer here.

Lastly, this book is also about my own enduring relationship with this special space and place, of small vignettes and ethnographic fragments and encounters, including of daily Goan village life, and contemplations of self and other. I also conceive of my ethnography as a form of research design unto itself, one that operates in simultaneity to Goa designing its heritage landscape (and sense of self) over a twenty-five-year time frame. Both are in flux, and always dynamic, always relational to one another. It is a form of 'patchwork ethnography' (following Gökçe Gunel, Saiba Varma, and Chika Watanabe) that carefully crafts itself through a multimodal range of techniques, involving traditional fieldwork methods, mapping as memory-making and storytelling, design work, curating and performance, and online research. The in-person and the online supplement one another and allow for an exploration of real and digital life-worlds through ideas of shared content and connection. Finally, my ethnography serves as an example of creating (and designing) a space for other community-based heritage voices not only to emerge, but also to be seen, heard, and listened to, visualized and written about. Like Frederick who runs Goa,1556 Press and believes that enduring arguments about Goa's uniqueness blunts and stunts useful comparison, I also very much want to counter Goa's exceptionalism, one based on its Portuguese colonial past and Indian present that then gets translated into its enduring historical, cultural, and religious difference. Even as Goa is distinctive in its heritage specificity (and is the product of a longue-durée melding or crossover of multiple European and Indian traits, including Catholic, Islamic, and Hindu influences), it also carries parallels with other places and spaces caught in 'in-between zones of civilization' (Feuchtwang and Rowlands 2019) and can be used as a productive site for thinking about both the generalizations and particulars of heritage and design landscapes. Here I am reminded of the way in which my in-depth, long-term research in Goa has helped me understand Zanzibar's layered heritage landscape as a form of the baroque (Gupta 2019a). In other words, I would like to suggest that the research design of this book on Goa could be used as an additional resource material for realizing and interpreting other innovative heritage design landscapes, both near and far.

References

Adamson, G. (2010). *The Craft Reader*. New York: Berg Press.

Ahmed, S. (2010). *The Promise of Happiness*. Durham, NC: Duke University Press.

Ali, M. (2006). *Alentejo Blue*. New York: Scribner.

Andrews, C. (2009). *Heritage Ethnography as a Specialized Craft: Grasping Maritime Heritage in Bermuda*. London: Routledge.

Appadurai, A. (2013). *The Future as Cultural Fact: Essays on the Global Condition*. London: Verso.

Augé, M. (1995). *Non-Places: An Introduction to Supermodernity*, trans. J. Howe. New York: Verso.

Bruner, E. (2001). 'Tourism in the Balinese Borderzone', in S. Lavie and T. Swedenburg, eds., *Displacement, Diaspora and Geographies of Identity*. Durham, NC: Duke University Press, pp. 157–80.

Butler, B. (2016). 'The Efficacies of Heritage: Syndromes, Magics, and Possessional Acts', *Public Archaeology* 15 (2–3): 113–35.

Cahen, M. (2012). '"Portugal Is in the Sky": Conceptual Considerations on Community, Lusitanity and Lusophony', in E. Morier-Genoud and M. Cahen, eds., *Imperial Migrations: Colonial Communities and Diaspora in the Portuguese World*. London: Palgrave Macmillan, pp. 297–315.

Chin, E. (2017). 'On Multimodal Anthropologies from the Space of Design: Toward Participant Making', *American Anthropologist* 119 (3): 541–3.

Clammer, J. R. (2012). *Culture, Development, and Social Theory: Towards an Integrated Social Development*. London: Zed Press.

Collins, S. G., Durington, M., and Gill, H. (2017). 'Multimodality: An Invitation', *American Anthropologist* 119 (1): 142–6.

Connell, R. (2007). *Southern Theory: The Global Dynamics of Knowledge in Social Science*. Cambridge: Polity Press.

Crick, M. (1989). 'Representations of International Tourism in the Social Sciences: Sun, Sex, Sights, Savings, and Servility', *Annual Review of Anthropology* 18: 307–44.

Da Cunha, G. (2004). 'Architect's Note', in *Museum of Houses of Goa*. Torda: Architecture Autonomous.

Da Cunha, G., ed. (2008). *Mario de Miranda*. Torda: Architecture Autonomous.

Da Cunha, G., ed. (2010a). *Inside Goa*. Torda: Architecture Autonomous.

Da Cunha, G., ed. (2010b). *Mario's Best Cartoons Book I*. Torda: Architecture Autonomous.

Da Cunha, G., ed. (2010c). *Mario's Best Cartoons Book II*. Torda: Architecture Autonomous.

Da Cunha, G., ed. (2010d). *Mario's Bombay*. Torda: Architecture Autonomous.

Da Cunha, G., ed. (2010e). *Mario's Goa*. Torda: Architecture Autonomous.

Da Cunha, G., ed. (2010f). *Mario's Travels*. Torda: Architecture Autonomous.

Da Cunha, G., ed. (2016a). *The Life of Mario, 1949*, trans. N. L. E. De Sousa. Torda: Architecture Autonomous.

Da Cunha, G., ed. (2016b). *The Life of Mario, 1950*, trans. N. L. E. De Sousa. Torda: Architecture Autonomous.

Da Cunha, G., ed. (2016c). *The Life of Mario, 1951*, trans. N. L. E. De Sousa. Torda: Architecture Autonomous.

Da Cunha, G., Pandit, H., and Mascarenhas, A., text; Koshy, A., photos (1999). *Houses of Goa*. Torda: Gerard da Cunha and Architecture Autonomous.

Dasgupta, P. (2009). *Edge of Faith*, essay by W. Dalrymple. Calcutta: Seagull Books.

Dattatreyan, E. G. and Marrero-Guillamón, I. (2019). 'Introduction: Multimodal Anthropology and the Politics of Invention', *American Anthropologist* 121: 220–8.

Di Giovine, M. (2009). *The Heritage-scape: UNESCO, World Heritage, and Tourism*. Lanham, MD: Lexington Books.

Escobar, A. (2018). *Designs for the Pluriverse: Radical Interdependence, Autonomy, and the Making of Worlds*. Durham, NC: Duke University Press.

Ezdani, Y. V. (2007). *Songs of the Survivors*. Saligao: Goa,1556.

Fernandes, D. (2012). *Mapusa, Yesterday and Today: A Reminiscent Tour*. Saligao: Goa,1556.

Fernandes, J. (2014). 'The Curious Case of Goan Orientalism', *ACT27 Goa Portuguesa*: 155–77.

Feuchtwang, S. and Rowlands, M. (2019). *Civilisation Recast: Theoretical and Historical Perspectives*. Cambridge: Cambridge University Press.

Fisher, E. (2014). *The Good Life: Aspiration, Dignity, and the Anthropology of Well Being*. Stanford, CA: Stanford University Press.

Frenz, M. (2014). *Community, Memory and Migration in a Globalizing World: The Goan Experience, c. 1890–1980*. New Delhi: Oxford University Press.

Ghosh, A. (2016). *The Great Derangement: Climate Change and the Unthinkable*. Chicago: University of Chicago Press.

Gracias, F. S. (2012). *Cozinha de Goa: History and Tradition of Goan Food*, 2nd ed. Saligao: Goa,1556.

Gupta, P. (2009a). 'The Disquieting of History: Portuguese Decolonization and Goan Migration in the Indian Ocean', *Journal of Asian and African Studies* 44(1): 19–48.

Gupta, P. (2009b). 'Goa, the Internal "Exotic" in South Asia: Discourses of Colonialism and Tourism', in A. Phukan and V. G. Rajan, eds., *Reading the Exotic, South Asia and Its Others*. Cambridge: Cambridge Scholars Press, pp. 123–48.

Gupta, P. (2014a). 'Frozen Vodka and White Skin in Tourist Goa', in D. Picard and M. Di Giovine, eds., *Tourism and the Power of Otherness: Seductions of Difference*. Bristol: Channel View Publications, pp. 95–109.

Gupta, P. (2014b). *The Relic State: St. Francis Xavier and the Politics of Ritual in Portuguese India*. Studies in Imperialism Series. Manchester: Manchester University Press.

Gupta, P. (2014c). 'Some (Not So) Lost Aquatic Traditions: Goans Going Fishing in the Indian Ocean', *Interventions* 16 (6): 854–76.

Gupta, P. (2015). 'The Virgin Herself', Review of Alinka Echeverria's *The Road to Tepeyac* (2010), *GoaPhoto 2015: The Other*. New Delhi: Naveen Printers, in partnership with The Alkazi Foundation for the Arts, pp. 42–4.

Gupta, P. (2016). 'Visuality and Diasporic Dynamism: Goans in Mozambique and Zanzibar', *African Studies* 75 (2): 257–77.

Gupta, P. (2017). 'The Corporeal and the Carnivalesque: The 2004 Exposition of St. Francis Xavier and the Consumption of History in Postcolonial Goa', *Etnográfica* 21 (1): 107–24.

Gupta, P. (2018a). 'Blue Johannesburg', in E. Boehmer and D. Davies, eds., *Planned Violence: Post/Colonial Urban Infrastructures, Literature and Culture*. London: Palgrave Macmillan, pp. 213–30.

Gupta, P. (2018b). 'Village Delhi', in K. Bystrom, A. Harris, and A. J. Webber, eds., *South and North: Contemporary Urban Orientations*. New York: Routledge, pp. 103–24.

Gupta, P. (2019a). 'Balcony, Door, Shutter: Baroque Heritage as Materiality and Biography in Stone Town, Zanzibar', Vienna Working Papers in Ethnography (VWPE no. 9, 2019). Department of Social and Cultural Anthropology, University of Vienna. www.ksa.univie.ac./vwpe09.

Gupta, P. (2019b). 'Being Goan Modern in Zanzibar: Mobility, Relationality and the Stitching of Race', in W. Anderson, R. Roque, and R. Ventura, eds., *Lusotropicalism and Its Discontents: The Making and Unmaking of Racial Exceptionalism in the Portuguese Speaking World*. New York: Berghahn Books, pp. 265–86.

Gupta, P. (2019c). *Portuguese Decolonization in the Indian Ocean World: History and Ethnography*. London: Bloomsbury Academic Press.

Gupta, P. (2019d). 'Renovating in Beira (Mozambique)', in *Portuguese Decolonization in the Indian Ocean World: History and Ethnography*. London: Bloomsbury Academic Press, pp. 127–44.

Gupta, P. (2021). 'Ways of Seeing Wetness', *Wasifiri* 36 (2): 37–47.

Gupta, P., Lee, C., Moorman, M., and Shukla, S., eds. (2018). 'Editors' Introduction' to 'The Global South: Histories, Politics, Maps', *Radical History Review* 131 (May): 1–12.

Hine, C. (2000). *Virtual Ethnography*. London: Sage.

Horst, H. and Miller, D. (2012). *Digital Anthropology*. Oxford: Berg.

Howes, D. (2004). *Empire of the Senses: The Sensual Cultural Reader*. Oxford: Berg.

Jackson, S. (2014). 'Rethinking Repair', in T. Gillespie, P.P Boczkowski, and K. Foot, eds., *Media Technologies: Essays on Communication, Materiality, and Society*. Cambridge, MA: MIT Press, pp. 221–39.

Kirshenblatt-Gimblett, B. (1998). *Destination Culture: Tourism, Museums, and Heritage*. Berkeley: University of California Press.

Korpela, M. (2013). 'Marginally Mobile? The Vulnerable Lifestyle of Westerners in Goa', *Dve domovini/Two Homelands* 38: 63–72.

Mac Dougall, L., ed. (2015). *GoaPhoto 2015: The Other*. New Delhi: Naveen Printers, in partnership with The Alkazi Foundation for the Arts.

Mac Dougall, L., ed. (2018). *GoaPhoto 2017: House Taken Over*. New Delhi: Mentecato Books.

Mazzarella, W. T. S. (2003). *Shoveling Smoke: Advertising and Globalization in Contemporary India*. Durham, NC: Duke University Press.

Meloy, E. (2002). *The Anthropology of Turquoise: Reflections on Desert and Sky*. New York: Vintage Books.

Metcalf, T. (2007). *Imperial Connections: India in the Indian Ocean Arena, 1860–1920*. Berkeley: University of California Press.

Meurs, P. (2016). *Heritage-Based Design*. Delft, Netherlands: Technology University Delft-Heritage and Architecture.

Miranda, M. (2001). *Goa with Love*, 3rd ed. Mumbai: M&M Publishers.

Nandy, A. (2007). 'An Ambiguous Journey to the City: The Village and Other Odd Ruins of the Self in the Indian Imagination', in *A Very Popular Exile*. Oxford: Oxford University Press.

Nelson, M. (2009). *Bluets*. Seattle: Wave Books.

Newman, R. (2001). *Of Umbrellas, Goddesses and Dreams: Essays on Goan Culture and Society*, Mapusa: Other India Press.

Newman, R. (2019a). *Goan Anthropology: Festivals, Films and Fish*. Saligao: Goa,1556.

Newman, R. (2019b). *Goan Anthropology: Mothers, Miracles and Mythology*. Saligao: Goa,1556.

Noronha, F. (2009). *Another Goa*. Saligao: Goa,1556.

Pandit, H. (2004). *Walking in Goa*. Muzaffarpur: Rekha Prakashan.

Pandit, H. (2008). *In and Around Old Goa*. Mumbai: The Marg Foundation.

Pandit, H. (2015). *There Is More to Life Than a House in Goa*. Delhi: Partridge India.

Pandit, H. and T. Rao (2006). *Walking With Angels*. Goa: Heritage Network.

Pandit, H. and F. Vakil (2003). *Hidden Hands: Master Builders of Goa*. Goa: Heritage Network.

Passos, J. (2012). 'Goa, O Mundo E As Artes Nas Caricaturas de Mario de Miranda', Universidade de Minho (Portugal), *XIII Coloquio de Otouno, Estetica, Cultura Material, e Dialogos Intersemioticos*, Organized by A. G. Macedo, C. M. de Sousa, and V. Moura.

Pink, S. (2009). *Doing Sensory Ethnography*. London: Sage.

Powell, M. (2011). 'Village Vibes', in H. D. Menezes and J. Lourenco, eds., *Inside/Out: New Writings from Goa*. Saligao: Goa,1556.

Prestholdt, J. (2008). *Domesticating the World: African Consumerism and the Genealogies of Globalization*. Berkeley: University of California Press.

Rodricks, W. (2012a). *The Green Room*. New Delhi: Rain Tree (Rupa Publications).

Rodricks, W. (2012b). *Moda Goa: History and Style*. New Delhi: Harper Collins India.

Rodricks, W. (2017). *Poskem: Goans in the Shadows*. Noida: Om Books.

Saldanha, A. (2007). *Psychedelic White: Goa Trance and the Viscosity of Race*. Minneapolis: University of Minnesota Press.

Sen, O. (1994). *River of Stories*. New Delhi: Kalpavriksh.

Sennett, R. (2008). *The Craftsman*. New Haven, CT: Yale University Press.

Solnit, R. (2005). *A Field Guide to Getting Lost*. New York: Penguin.

Trichur, R. (2000). 'Politics of Goan Historiography', *Lusotopie* 2000: 637–46.

Trichur, R. (2013). *Refiguring Goa: From Trading Post to Tourism Destination*. Saligao: Goa,1556.

Viegas, S. (2011). *Let Me Tell You About Quinta*. New Delhi: Penguin.

Viegas, S. (2018). *Song Sung Blue*. Fatorda, Goa: Saxtti Foundation.

Interviews:

Da Cunha, Gerard. January and February 2000; 29 November 2013; 27 May 2019. Goa, India.

D'Souza, Arvind. 4 June 2019. Goa, India.

Jon, Savio. 10 January 2014; 7 June 2019. Goa, India.

Kapur, Diviya. August–December 2013; 7 September 2013; 19 February 2018. Goa, India.

Kerkar, Subodh. May–June 2019. Goa, India.

Mac Dougall, Lola. August–December 2013; 25 February–7 March 2015; 17–27 November 2017; April–June 2019. Goa, India.

Mendes, Sacha. 18 December 2013; conversations in 2015, 2017, 2018; 7 June 2019. Goa, India.

Noronha, Frederick. 24 November 2017; 5 June 2019. Goa, India.

Rodricks, Wendell. 23 November 2013. Goa, India.

Sen, Orijit. August–December 2013; May 2019. Goa, India.

Siqueira, Alito. August–November 2013. Goa, India.

Viegas, Savia. 30 May 2019. Goa, India.

Online Source Materials

Section 1

www.culanth.org/fieldsights/series/keywords-for-ethnography-and-design

www.culanth.org/fieldsights/a-manifesto-for-patchwork-ethnography

www.abc.net.au/radionational/programs/archived/bydesign/2008-08-23/3200730

Section 2

www.xchr.in

www.tajhotels.com/en-in/taj/taj-fort-aguada-goa/

https://thecrowngoa.com/

http://whatsupgoa.com/cafechocolatti/

http://goanet.org

www.modagoamuseum.org/

Section 3

https://mappingmapusamarket.wordpress.com

www.serendipityartsfestival.com/

https://kochimuzirisbiennale.org/

www.peopletreeonline.com

www.scroll.in/latest/880649/french-brand-christian-dior-settles-plagiarism-dispute-with-indian-design-studio-people-tree/

www.kochimuzirisbiennale.org/lets-talk-with-orijit-sen/

www.heraldgoa.in/Cafe/Mapusa-market-Splendidly-graphic/124151.html

Section 4

www.wendellrodricks.com/i/moda-goa-museum-research-centre
www.nytimes.com/2019/03/30/fashion/museum-costume-goa-india.html
www.modagoamuseum.org
www.saviojon.com/
http://elle.in/fashion/designer-savio-jon-interview/
https://tamil-table.business.site/

Section 5
www.literati-goa.com/
www.amitavghosh.com/
www.goanet.org/
www.goa1556.in/about-goa-1556/
www.xchr.in

Section 6
www.archgoa.org
www.reismagosfort.com
www.intach.org
www.telegraph.co.uk/news/worldnews/asia/india/1413458/Tycoons-widow-loses-battle-to-restore-Goas-ancient-fort.html
https://timesofindia.indiatimes.com/city/goa/Reis-Magos-fort-Plea-on-JMFC-order-rejected/articleshow/3943128.cms
https://mumbaimirror.indiatimes.com/news/india/not-with-british-cash-sena/articleshow/15833299.cms
https://economictimes.indiatimes.com/news/politics-and-nation/shiv-sena-objects-govts-move-to-beautify-reis-magos-fort/articleshow/3256084.cms
www.navhindtimes.com/story.php?story=2009020114
https://timesofindia.indiatimes.com/city/goa/Restored-at-3-5-crore-Reis-Magos-fort-opens/articleshow/13858603.cms
www.bbc.com/news/world-asia-india-36220327
www.mariodemiranda.com
www.incrediblegoa.org/focus/goas-adil-shah-palace-gets-complete-facelift-serendipity-art-festival/

Section 7
www.facebook.com/littlexanti/
www.goaphoto.in
www.goaphoto.in/2015/
www.goaphoto.in/2017/
www.goaphoto.in/2019/
www.museumofgoa.com/

www.goachitra.com/

https://lbb.in/goa/plum-cake-eclairs-jila-bakery/

www.saviaviegas.in/painting.html

www.saviaviegas.in/gita_chadha.html

https://scroll.in/article/923000/this-dark-tale-from-goa-told-in-words-and-pictures-
    is-made-less-menacing-by-detached-storytelling

www.joaoroqueliteraryjournal.com/review-events-new/2019/5/20/song-sung-blue-
    by-savia-viegas

www.joaoroqueliteraryjournal.com/nonfiction-1/2019/2/18/mz9x48s8rbvqi6io
    nmxbjliyo6l36a

www.saviaviegas.in

Acknowledgements

This book is the product of a twenty-five-year period of visiting Goa, for longer and shorter durations, as I travelled the world and came into my own, from first being a young PhD student based in the USA to becoming a professor of anthropology based in South Africa. It is a love of place that motivated me to write this small book and endures. It will also forever be my lockdown book, a first draft of which anchored me during those hard months of March until May 2020 when we all took shelter at home from the little-known Covid pandemic that was fast travelling the globe. I would like to thank Juan and Padma for sharing their love of Goa with me and creating a lively sense of family during these difficult past two years that also witnessed the loss of both my parents.

The writing of this book would not have been possible without the generosity and candidness of those who agreed to spend such invaluable time with me – talking about Goa's lively heritage, opening up about their design inspirations, and becoming the set of portraits sketched here. I would like to give a special thanks to Orijit Sen, Savio Jon, Wendell Rodricks (late), Sacha Mendes, Diviya Kapur, Frederick Noronha, Gerard Da Cunha, Lola Mac Dougall, Savia Viegas, Arvind D'Souza, Mario Miranda (late), Vandana Naik, Maria de Fatima Figueiredo de Albuquerque, Monika Ghurde (late), Aradhana Seth, Amitav Ghosh, Subodh Kerkar, Rukshana Sarosh, Nazneen Sarosh, and Ricardo Rebelo. Even as I missed crossing paths this time around with Heta Pandit, her important writings on Goa's heritage were also a guiding path for my own. A special thank you to Orijit for contributing the wonderful set of illustrations that accompany my text and honour the creative individuals showcased here. I most grateful Alito Siqueira for his generosity and scholarship. A sociologist by training based at Goa University, he tragically passed away in August 2019. He helped inspire this book project and two generations of scholars writing on Goa from inside and abroad.

I would like to thank my colleagues on the animated WiSER corridor in Johannesburg that has been my academic home for the last fifteen years: Sarah Nuttall, Achille Mbembe, Adila Deshmukh, Najibha Deshmukh, Hlonipha Mokoena, Jonathan Klaaren, Keith Breckenridge, Isabel Hofmeyr, and Richard Rottenburg. I am also grateful to be a recipient of a South Africa's National Research Fund CPRR grant entitled 'Island Futures and Design Ethnography in the Indian Ocean', which helped fund my fieldwork visits to Goa during 2017 to 2019.

Lastly, I would like to extend a special thanks to my enduring Goa family, who always welcome me back with each and every visit and quickly involve me in their Goa world(s): Rukshana, Naz, and their mum, Ricardo, Rhea, and Karsh, and Sangeeta and Rajesh.

Cambridge Elements ☰

Critical Heritage Studies

Kristian Kristiansen
University of Gothenburg

Michael Rowlands
UCL

Francis Nyamnjoh
University of Cape Town

Astrid Swenson
Bath University

Shu-Li Wang
Academia Sinica

Ola Wetterberg
University of Gothenburg

About the Series

This series focuses on the recently established field of Critical Heritage Studies. Interdisciplinary in character, it brings together contributions from experts working in a range of fields, including cultural management, anthropology, archaeology, politics, and law. The series will include volumes that demonstrate the impact of contemporary theoretical discourses on heritage found throughout the world, raising awareness of the acute relevance of critically analysing and understanding the way heritage is used today to form new futures.

Cambridge Elements ≡

Critical Heritage Studies